Fix Overthinking in Relationships

ELIMINATE TOXIC THOUGHTS, STOP SABOTAGING YOUR RELATIONSHIPS, KEEP YOUR SANITY, AND FEEL MORE CONNECTED TO YOUR PARTNER

EDGAR WISE

Copyright 2023 by Edgar Wise

All rights reserved.

The content contained within this book may not be reproduced, duplicated or transmitted without direct written permission from the author or the publisher.

Under no circumstances will any blame or legal responsibility be held against the publisher, or author, for any damages, reparation, or monetary loss due to the information contained within this book, either directly or indirectly.

Legal Notice:

This book is copyright protected. It is only for personal use. You cannot amend, distribute, sell, use, quote or paraphrase any part, or the content within this book, without the consent of the author or publisher.

Disclaimer Notice:

Please note the information contained within this document is for educational and entertainment purposes only. All effort has been executed to present accurate, up to date, reliable, complete information. No warranties of any kind are declared or implied. Readers acknowledge that the author is not engaged in the rendering of legal, financial, medical or professional advice. The content within this book has been derived from various sources. Please consult a licensed professional before attempting any techniques outlined in this book.

By reading this document, the reader agrees that under no circumstances is the author responsible for any losses, direct or indirect, that are incurred as a result of the use of the information contained within this document, including, but not limited to, errors, omissions, or inaccuracies.

Contents

Bonus Ebooks — 1

Introduction — 3

Chapter 1: The Root Causes of Overthinking in a Relationship — 7

Chapter 2: The Impact of Overthinking on a Person's Health and Well-Being — 23

Chapter 3: Understanding Relationship Rumination — 35

Chapter 4: Importance of Self-Awareness in a Relationship — 47

Chapter 5: Strategies for Overcoming Overthinking in Relationships — 63

Chapter 6: Prioritizing Achieving Happiness in Relationships — 87

Chapter 7: How to End a Toxic Relationship — 101

Conclusion — 115

About the Author — 121

Leaving a Review 123

References 125

Bonus Ebooks

Scan QR Code Below

https://edgarwise.com

Introduction

Anxiety can be a debilitating thing to deal with at the best of times. It can quickly cause your peace of mind to evaporate and affect your life in all manner of ways. It can keep you from concentrating on your work, for instance, and mess with the quality of work you are doing. It can cause you to become distracted when you are out with your friends and family. Most importantly, though, it can deal significant blows to your relationships by making your mind spiral in every which direction. Small moments suddenly get blown out of proportion, and minor mistakes or errors keep replaying in your mind. They get fixed in your mind's eye, causing you embarrassment all over again, chipping away at your self-confidence, and making you think that people are judging you or laughing at you, or simply do not want to be around you. Even when that is not even close to being the case.

If you are an anxious person prone to overthinking, such scenarios are probably familiar to you. You might have experienced how damaging overthinking can be to your relationships at work, school, or just life in general. You might even recognize it as a problem, without knowing if there is a solution to it, a way out. Luckily, there is. Stopping your negative thoughts from swirling around and around in your mind might be challenging to do at first and later, from time to time, but it is not impossible. Trying to understand what other people are really thinking may be challenging, especially if the person in question is a partner who is not on the same page as you. But it is a challenge that can be overcome and mastered, so long as you know how, and that "how" is exactly what you will discover in *Fix Overthinking in Relationships*.

Fix Overthinking in Relationships is all about providing you with the toolkit you need to address and overcome the most common issues associated with overthinking in relationships. It shows you how to deal with all sorts of anxieties, from relationship worries to rumination, and supplies you with the approaches, techniques, tips, expert advice, and real-life stories you need to do so. In short, the book you are currently holding in your hand is designed to help you train your mind to stop overthinking and actually start enjoying the relationships you are in.

Seeing a way out of your anxieties can be very hard to do when you are stuck in anxious loops overthinking. But there are actually many different tools you can use, like nurturing positivity, mindfulness practices, clear communication skills, and self-awareness techniques to break those loops. In other words, there are a number of things you can do to break free and create stronger, more meaningful connections with the people in your life. With that in mind, are you ready to begin?

Chapter 1

The Root Causes of Overthinking in a Relationship

Before we can begin talking about all the different techniques you can use to overcome overthinking, we must first understand what overthinking really is and where it comes from. Trying to overcome overthinking without understanding its root cause would be a bit like putting a Band-Aid over a deep wound that really needs stitching. True, you may have covered up the initial laceration, but because you are not addressing the tear and damage beneath the skin, you will not be able to stop the bleeding. Similarly, you have to understand what the signs of overthinking are.

As bizarre as this might sound, overthinking is not always something that is easy to recognize, especially once it has turned into a habit. Habits are a bit like reflexes, after all. You do not really have to think about them to execute them. If a ball is flying toward your face, you do not think about raising your arms to protect yourself. You just do it. Going back to the whole "wound" analogy from a moment ago, you can liken overthinking to an internal wound. You might not be bleeding on the outside, but inside something might be very wrong and, therefore, causing you a great deal of pain. Even if you do not immediately realize it. Understanding what the signs of overthinking are, then, can make you see when you are experiencing it. Having recognized that you are overthinking things, you can press that big, red "STOP" button in your mind and change your patterns of thinking.

Understanding Relationship Anxiety: Root of Overthinking in a Relationship

A lot of people believe that thoughts are just something that happens to us. They seem to think that our thoughts come to us when and where they please, flitting in and out of our minds seemingly at random. This, however, could not be farther from the truth. We have a lot more control over our thoughts and how they affect us than we think we do. We might not be able to control every single little thought that pops into our minds, but we have the power to choose which ones to follow after. Before going into that in greater detail, though, let's first understand where thoughts come from.

While scientists haven't been able to figure out how, precisely, thoughts are formed, they do know that they are the result of things they refer to as distal and proximal causes. Distal causes are things we have experienced in our past, which color our expectations and prime our emotions and thoughts. For instance, if your first experience with a dog involves being badly bitten, then you will likely feel a spike of fear when you see a big dog coming towards you and your first thought will be, "I need to get away." The proximal causes, on the other hand, are the external stimuli you get from the environment and situation you are in. Such factors understandably impact how we feel, both on a physical and emotional level, color our mood, and, again, our thoughts. If you are in a really crowded space, on a very hot day, without any air conditioning, for example, you will feel sweaty, cramped, and uncomfortable. These sensations will make you irritable and annoyed, which might make you think, "I hate being here."

So, why is all this important in the context of overthinking? Well, overthinking is often related to anxiety and anxiety can be triggered by a variety of factors. Let's say you used to be in a relationship and your previous partner cheated on you. Now, you are in a new relationship with a new partner, and you have noticed that they've been really busy lately. Since your previous experience with a partner who was "always busy" meant that they were cheating on you, this situation can trigger your anxiety. Your anxiety can then trigger certain thoughts that start running in a loop in your mind. "What if I'm being cheated on again?" you might find yourself asking. Before you know it, you might end up replaying cheating scenarios in your mind, when really your partner is just stuck in the office, working on a boring report.

If you want to stop overthinking and keep it from damaging your relationship—by emotionally distancing yourself from your partner who's stuck in their office, because you have convinced yourself they are cheating on you, for instance—then you need to understand where this habit comes from. You know that overthinking is a result of relationship anxiety. But what is the root cause of that anxiety? While you will have specific reasons that fuel your anxiety, these reasons will typically be related to one of four things (Plumptree, 2022):

- negative past experiences

- having an anxious attachment style

- low self-esteem

- poor communication skills

If you had a cheating ex-partner, then clearly the root cause of your anxiety and overthinking are your negative past experiences. What about having an anxious attachment style, though? What exactly does that mean? Imagine a scenario where you are constantly questioning your partner's feelings for you. You are constantly asking yourself if they care about you as much as you care about them, and these questions keep plaguing you day and night. A lot of the time, this kind of situation can be traced all the way back to your childhood. If, say, you grew up with parents and guardians who did not show you much attention or love, if they were not particularly caring and consistently there for you? Then the kind of environment you grew up in has probably affected your need for affection. Growing up with people who were affectionate one moment and distant and unapproachable the next can cause you to develop a mindset where you constantly need to be reassured that the people you love, love you back.

This mindset is something that you can easily carry into your adult relationships in later years. For example, let's say you have developed an anxious attachment style and your partner is busy trying to finish an important project that week. As a result, they are not able to show you as much attention and affection as they normally could have. In such a case, your mind can go into "overthink" mode instead of understanding that the situation is due to their work. You might start equating their inability to pay attention to you with how much they care for you, even if you grasp how important their project is on a surface level. The anxiety you feel because of your attachment style can override your logical thinking capabilities and thus, make your thoughts spiral.

Low self-esteem, meanwhile, is another root cause of anxiety and overthinking. Low self-esteem can easily stop you from seeing the value in yourself. This can in turn cause you to question the feelings other people have for you. I mean, how can you believe people see value in you if you are unable to value yourself in the first place? Low self-esteem and the resultant mentality, then, can cause you to disbelieve other people's thoughts and opinions of you. You might dismiss the genuine compliments that your partner gives you, for instance. You might become swept away by thoughts like, "I do not deserve them," or "What do they even see in me?"

A final cause of overthinking is poor communication skills. A lot of the time, we end up overthinking past arguments and incidents and worry about how they feel about us because we did not communicate our feelings and needs to them when we should have. Say that your partner did something to hurt you, but you did not tell them their behavior hurt you. Maybe you just expected them to know. Maybe you did not want to hurt their feelings by telling them they hurt yours.

Whatever the case may be, choosing not to share something, like your feelings, thoughts or worries is a sure way to get them to start festering in you. The same goes for your need to talk about the state of your relationship, the future, or anything else that may be on your mind. You might be hesitant to bring up such things because you worry that it is too early to do so. But have to remember that keeping things bottled up when you should be expressing them to your partner will not benefit the relationship. Instead, it'll cause you to overthink even the most minute things and put chinks in your relationship.

Signs of Relationship Anxiety

Relationship anxiety can manifest itself in a variety of different ways. So can overthinking. Given that, recognizing anxiety and overthinking what they are can be rather difficult. The good news is that you learn to recognize both by understanding what exactly you need to watch out for. Once you do, you can spot it when you are becoming anxious and keep yourself from becoming stuck in loops of overthinking. You can also prevent the typical problems that unaddressed relationship anxiety can lead to such as emotional distress, emotional exhaustion, physical health problems, and lack of motivation.

- **Constantly seeking reassurance.**
  One of the most obvious signs of overthinking is excessively seeking reassurance (Caporuscio, 2020). This can manifest itself in many ways. You might find yourself constantly asking questions like "Are you there for me?" and "Do I really matter to you?" or "Do you really love me?" and expecting your partner to keep reassuring you. These reassurances, though, will only work in the very short term, if they work at all. They will not quiet down the anxiety you are feeling, because they will not address its root cause. In this case, the root cause will be inherently believing that your partner will not actually miss you if you were to leave, that they are just with you because it is convenient, or because of all the different things you do for them (Raypole, 2019). It can even make you conclude that your partner would not support or help you if you needed them to. This can in turn keep you from asking for support and help which will further erode your relationship and increase your anxiety.

- **Doubting how your partner feels about you.**
  Another way relationship anxiety manifests is not believing that your partner really loves you or cares about you. This results in your looking at their behavior and interpreting the things they do or do not do in this light.

It prevents you from considering, for instance, that the reason your partner might be acting or not acting a certain way is that their love language is different from your own. It keeps you from interpreting things like how slow they are in responding to your texts, not as them being busy, but as them wanting to avoid you. Anxiety manifesting in this way causes you to interpret every little change in behavior, every time your partner appears remotely distant as a validation of your fears.

- **Doubting how compatible the two of you really are.** Relationship anxiety often causes you to question how compatible you and your partner are in the long term. This happens more when you get into an argument or have a disagreement of some sort, of course, but it can also happen when things are going perfectly well. It can result in your questioning whether you actually want to be with your partner and whether or not you are actually happy. It can even make you blow very minor differences, like having different tastes in movies or books, way out of proportion and use them as evidence showing how incompatible the two of you really are.

- **Frequently worrying that your partner is going to break up with you.** On the flip side, relationship anxiety can express itself as worries that your partner will break up with you. The mark of a good relationship is one where you feel safe, secure, happy, and loved. This manifestation of anxiety, however, can prevent you from feeling these things in your relationship. This is especially true in cases where these worries evolve into a constant nagging fear, driving you to analyze your partner's behavior, down to the most minute of actions, looking for signs that they are ready to walk away. The thing is, this fear can start coloring your attitude and guiding your behavior which damages your relationship more by keeping you from discussing important relationship issues that need to be addressed or turning a blind eye to the things that your partner does that bother you, rather than addressing them. Left unchecked such fear-guided behavior can cause the relationship to become brittle enough to snap, causing your partner to actually end things with you.

- **Sabotaging your own relationships.**
A very interesting sign that you are experiencing relationship anxiety is trying to sabotage the relationship you are in. This does not mean intentionally sabotaging your relationship, of course. Rather it is doing so subconsciously, without even realizing it. A person with relationship anxiety can sabotage their relationships to test them and how much their partner apparently cares about them. For instance, shutting them out emotionally and then concluding that they do not understand you would count as relationship sabotage. So would pushing them away and deciding that they do not care enough about you to close the gap. The typical behavior that people engage in when they sabotage their relationships is pushing their partners

away when they need their support, testing their partner's and the relationship's boundaries, and finding reasons to pick arguments with their partner.

- **Ignoring or not paying attention to the good moments.**
  People who have relationship anxiety tend to focus too much on negative things like arguments, stressful situations, and relationship conflict. They become blind to the good parts of the relationships or else start discounting them. A good way to see if you are exhibiting this sign is to observe your own thought patterns. Are you spending more time worrying about your relationships than you are enjoying them? If so, then you probably have a good deal of anxiety.

- **Misinterpreting their partner's actions.**
  A final sign that a person is suffering from relationship anxiety is frequently misinterpreting or mistreating their partner's words and actions. This kind of behavior attributes different motives to a partner's words and behavior than the ones they had meant. These motives often are more negative than their partner's actual motives. If you are engaging in this pattern of behavior and your partner is being taciturn because they had a bad day at work, you may interpret their behavior as their not wanting to spend any time with you.

What Causes Relationship Anxiety?

Now that you know what the various signs of relationship anxiety are, you might be wondering, "What causes relationship anxiety in the first place?" This kind of anxiety actually has several different root causes. Understanding these root causes is very important, because only by understanding them can you start addressing them. By addressing the root causes of your anxiety, you can start resolving them. By resolving the root causes of your anxiety, you can at last begin to alleviate it and thus, reduce and later completely eliminate your tendency to overthink.

One of the prime causes of relationship anxiety is low self-esteem. Your self-esteem is essentially the confidence you have in your own sense of worth and in your abilities and capabilities. Self-esteem is critical for your self-image, because it impacts various things like your self-respect, self-love, and self-compassion. When you have low self-esteem, you end up having low self-respect, self-love, and self-compassion as well (therapist.com team, 2022). As a result, you start believing that you are less worthy of other people's respect, love, and compassion, even your partners. As a result, you doubt your partner's feelings for you, even when they constantly reassure you of them (Murray et al., 1998). Psychologists refer to this phenomenon as projection and it can cause your relationship anxiety and a tendency to overthink significantly and interfere with your peace of mind.

Another, very obvious cause of relationship anxiety is negative experiences. If you had a partner that cheated on you, treated you poorly, dumped you out of the blue, lied about how they felt about you, misled you about your relationship status and what you were to them, or engaged in another, similar kind of damaging behavior, then those negative experiences will color your present reality. They will put you on edge and keep you from fully believing or trusting your current partner's words, actions, and feelings. They will put you in a state of mind where you are constantly waiting for the other shoe to drop.

Negative experiences may also cause you to develop certain triggers. Your anxiety will likely kick into overdrive when you encounter one of these triggers, causing you to spiral.

While questioning the nature of things is a human habit that can be beneficial in some situations—like if you are a scientist trying to prove a theorem—it can be quite damaging within the context of a relationship, if you overdo it. A questioning nature can cause you to question the reality and nature of your relationship frequently. This can cause you to doubt your and your partner's feelings and make it difficult for you to trust them. As you will see later, trust is the opposite of anxiety. Relationship anxiety cannot exist where relationship trust is and vice versa.

A final, but very important cause of relationship anxiety is the kind of attachment style you have. Your attachment style is the way you form bonds with other people (Raypole, 2019a). This includes everyone from your partner to your parents, your friends to your children. Your attachment style is typically formed and developed in childhood, mostly through your relationship with your parents, guardians, or caregivers.

Attachment styles fall into one of two categories: secure and insecure. As you might have surmised from those names, secure attachment styles are healthy ones, where you feel confident and secure in the relationships you are in. These feelings result in healthy relationships, where you experience little to no relationship anxiety. Insecure attachment styles, meanwhile, prevent you from feeling secure and confident in your relationships. You develop insecure attachment styles when your parents or caregivers were not able or willing to respond to your emotional needs while you were growing up. They develop as a result of you not having received the support and love you needed, which subconsciously gave you the message "you are not cared for" or "you cannot rely on the ones you love."

These messages, ingrained as they are in your psyche, can cause you to experience a significant amount of relationship anxiety. This is because they result in you not trusting your partner's feelings or trusting that they will be there for you in your time of need. There are two kinds of insecure attachment styles that might contribute to your relationship anxiety. These are (Raypole, 2019b):

- anxious attachment: You constantly worry that your partner will leave you because you have been left or abandoned—physically or emotionally—in the past.

- avoidant attachment: The level of intimacy and commitment you experience in a relationship stresses you out and worries you because you are either unused to it or you have subconsciously learned not to trust it.

Understanding the root causes of your relationship anxiety is key to alleviating it and putting an end to your overthinking habits. Once you know what's causing these two things, you can put in the necessary work to solve them. Resolve the cause and you will have resolved the issue, after all. Before diving deeper into how you can resolve the root causes of your relationship anxiety, and employ various other strategies to soothe your overthinking habit, let's take a closer look at how overthinking really affects you.

Key Takeaways

- Overthinking is usually connected to anxiety, and this can be provoked by a variety of factors.

- While the reasons for your anxiety can be multifaceted, they usually fall under one of four categories.: negative past experiences, having an anxious attachment style, low self-esteem, and poor communication skills.

- While it can be tough to pinpoint anxiety and excessive rumination, you can become better aware of the signs by familiarizing yourself with what to look out for.

- To help put an end to your overthinking and anxiety in relationships, it is essential that you identify the root causes of your worries.

- Knowing the signs of relationship anxiety can prevent

typical problems such as emotional distress, emotional exhaustion, physical health problems, and lack of motivation.

Chapter 2

The Impact of Overthinking on a Person's Health and Well-Being

You might be thinking that overthinking is just a mild problem, rather than a major issue. Perhaps you believe that it's not a significant matter and can continue to disregard it, as you've been doing for some time. You even recognize that overthinking is a problem for you, but treat it as something you can tend to at a later date since you do not have the time for it now.

The thing is, though, overthinking is actually a much bigger problem than most people give it credit for. Just because you have gotten used to overthinking does not mean it is not affecting you poorly. It just means you have become accustomed to just how overthinking affects you. Considering how badly overthinking can affect both your physical and your mental health, that is not exactly a good thing.

That overthinking can significantly damage your mental health should be fairly obvious to you when you think about it. That it is equally as damaging to your physical health, though may be news to you. However, that will not make this fact any less true. Overthinking can impact all sorts of things, like your cardiovascular system, brain, sleep patterns, and more.

Overthinking and Your Physical Health

Overthinking is the result of chronic, that is to say, constant anxiety. Anxiety affects your body in some very specific ways. It increases your heart rate and breathing and reduces blood flow to certain areas of the body while pumping more of it to others. This is because anxiety and stress are part of our survival mechanisms of yore. Back in the stone age, human beings would become stressed and anxious when they were under threat. If there was a predator in the region, for instance, they would be stressed and anxious. Their heart rate would increase to pump more blood to their extremities, meaning their arms and legs, so that they could run away. More blood would also be pumped to their brain, so they can be more alert and react more quickly. At the same time, less blood would be pumped into other areas of their body, like their digestive tract and their stomach.

Today, we still have the ability to become stressed and anxious. There is no problem with this in the short term. In the long term, though, this can become quite problematic. Prolonged stress and anxiety, and therefore prolonged overthinking, results in your heart constantly beating fast. The more you overthink, the more you fuel your stress and anxiety. The more you fuel your stress and anxiety, the more tired your heart and cardiovascular system become. The more tired your cardiovascular system becomes, the higher your risk of heart disease will be.

Don't believe me? Well, then, you should know that it is a proven fact that overthinking can lead to high blood pressure (Mishra, 2021). Your blood pressure is the pressure that your blood exerts on the inner walls of your veins as it is passing through them. Blood pressure that is constantly high is problematic because it wears the veins down, as well as the heart. Over time, this wear and tear accumulate and can lead to heart attacks or strokes (Gupta, 2022). At the same time, high blood pressure equals high cholesterol. High cholesterol can cause fatty deposits to accumulate in your veins. These can make it harder for blood to get through your veins over time, which can, again, lead to heart attacks and strokes (Mayo Clinic, 2021).

But overthinking does not just badly affect your heart and cardiovascular system. It physically affects your brain as well. It does this by overtiring your brain cells, which thus become incapable of working as they should. When overthinking goes on for long enough, it can actually start killing off brain cells (Mishra, 2021). This is one reason why overthinking affects your problem-solving skills and ability to make decisions, but more on that later.

Moving on, overthinking can also impact your digestive system. Remember how anxiety and stress divert blood flow and thus oxygen from your digestive system? Well, this has certain consequences, if it goes on for long enough. The chronic stress you experience, fueled as it is by overthinking, can result in a condition known as inflammatory bowel disease, otherwise known as IBD (Mayo Clinic, n.d.). IBD is a condition where your bowels literally become inflamed. This inflammation results in diarrhea, abdominal pain, blood in your stool, chronic fatigue, and a loss of appetite. Alternatively, overthinking can also result in your developing irritable bowel syndrome (IBS). This is a chronic condition that leads to cramping, constipation or diarrhea and bloating. Typically, IBS will go away when you are less stressed for a period of time but come back when you overthink, stress and anxiety levels spike (National Health Service, 2017).

Given the ways in which overthinking can affect your digestive system, it should not be surprising to find out that it can significantly reduce your appetite as well. This both has to do with how it affects your digestive system and how it affects your brain. After all, you are not very likely to get very hungry when your stomach's cramping, like you. But what does your brain have to do with your appetite? Plenty, because your brain is the organ that gives your body the "I'm hungry, feed me," signals.

In other words, it is the organ in charge of managing your appetite. It can't do that, however, if it is constantly busy tending to other things, like worrying about the state of your relationship. The amount of energy and time your brain devotes to overthinking, then, can keep your neurons from passing the necessary "I'm hungry, feed me," signals along. This can result in losing your appetite, which can cause you to lose weight on top of that.

Overthinking can interfere with your sleep patterns, the quality of your sleep, and its duration too (Mishra, 2021). Overthinking habits tend to peak when you are getting ready for bed and trying to sleep. This is because people might be able to distract themselves with all their chores and responsibilities during the day, but are unable to do so at night. How can they, when all these thoughts start rushing into their minds like they were waiting for things to quiet down? When this happens, anxiety and stress levels spike, making sleep a major challenge, if not an impossibility (Osborn, 2020).

If your overthinking habits interfere with your sleep, then that will mean you are not getting enough rest. You therefore will not be able to recharge your energy levels or be as clear-headed as you could have been. It will further mean that your immune system will become weaker, because the amount of sleep we get is directly related to the strength of our immune system, believe it or not (Olson, 2018).

Given all these facts, it should not be surprising to discover that overthinking can weaken your immune system. This is because your brain releases a hormone known as cortisol when you engage in overthinking. Cortisol is a stress hormone that lowers the immune system's effectiveness. In the short term, this does not matter. In the long term, meaning when you are overthinking all day every day, though, it can mean a great deal. After all, a weaker immune system will mean a reduced ability to fight off germs and diseases. A reduced ability to fight off diseases will mean getting sick more and being slower to recover from illnesses (Dr. Batra, n.d.).

A final way overthinking can impact your physical health can actually be observed in your hair and skin. Stress and anxiety, which are closely associated with overthinking as you now know, are known to cause inflammation throughout the body. You already saw an example of this when we were talking about the digestive tract. But your bowels are not the only part of your body that can become inflamed when you are stressed. Your skin can become inflamed as well, which can lead to rashes and flare-ups. The reason for this is that stress affects your endocrine system, meaning your network of glands and organs. This leads to all kinds of skin conditions, such as psoriasis and eczema. Put simply then, overthinking can literally manifest itself on your skin and your scalp, almost as though the negative thought loops you are stuck in are trying to express themselves there.

Overthinking and Your Mental Health

That was how overthinking affects your physical health. But what about your mental health and well-being? Considering the relationship between overthinking and anxiety, and overthinking, it can aptly be said that overthinking can impact your mental health as well. Psychologists often associate overthinking with Generalized Anxiety Disorder (GAD) and even depression.

Generalized Anxiety Disorder is a condition where the individual worries excessively about situations and issues every single day. Within the context of relationship anxieties, these worries can concern your partner's feelings, doubts you have about a relationship, the state or longevity of a relationship, and more (Cleveland Clinic, 2022). Individuals who develop GAD are usually swept away by their worries, anxieties, and fears for at least six months. They also find controlling their anxiety to be very difficult, which wreaks havoc on their peace of mind.

When you engage in overthinking and let your anxieties take over, you end up weakening your problem-solving skills, whether you have developed GAD or not. Anxiety is something that narrows your point of view. It prevents creative thinking and thus blinds to new avenues of thought. The problems you are struggling with thus start to seem insurmountable, which only adds to how stressed you feel and fuels your negative thought patterns (Stephanie, 2022).

One reason this happens is that overthinking exhausts the part of your brain that is in charge of creative problem-solving (Walsh, 2016). Another is that it wears our decision-making capabilities down and even causes something known as "decision fatigue," which makes taking action to address the source of your anxiety—say, a relationship problem you want to solve—much harder than it should be. Overthinking, then, reduces your ability to make good decisions. It also interferes with your ability to make decisions in a timely manner, by costing you a lot of time, which you may be spending playing through scenarios in your head that likely will not happen.

All of this naturally only exacerbates the anxiety that you are feeling. That overthinking, which is caused by relationship anxiety, can increase your anxiety means there is a cyclical relationship between anxiety and overthinking. The two feed off one another in a sort of positive feedback loop. This has dire consequences for your mental health because anxiety is known to (Mayo Clinic, 2018):

- feel tense, nervous, or restless continually.
- have trouble focusing or concentrating on what you are doing and on the present moment.
- interfere with your sleep and the quality of your sleep.
- cause you to experience panic attacks.
- feel constantly fatigued or tired.
- withdraw from friends and loved ones.
- experience a significant amount of loneliness.
- lower your mood.
- make you feel disconnected from the world and people around you.

The negative thoughts and feelings you experience when engaged in overthinking can easily lead to depression, as mentioned before. Depression is a mental health condition that causes overwhelming feelings of sadness and even hopelessness to the person going through it (Torres, 2020). Like with anxiety, overthinking and depression have a cyclical relationship in that they fuel one another. This is deeply problematic because depression can cause you to:

- lose interest in activities that you used to enjoy doing.
- become less energetic and feel like you are tired or fatigued all the time.
- lose your appetite, thereby leading to weight loss issues.
- overeat, thereby leading to sudden weight gain issues.
- have trouble falling asleep and suffer from poor quality of sleep.
- struggle with staying asleep throughout the night.
- act more lethargic and generally slower.
- feel guilty or worthless for no apparent reason.
- have more difficulty focusing on things.
- struggle with making decisions.
- start having suicidal thoughts.

Scientists running a study have observed that people who are clinically depressed tend to engage in overthinking more than people who have not been diagnosed with depression (Alloway, 2022). The same scientists have also discovered that individuals who become depressed engage in overthinking a great deal more than they used to before they develop a depressive mood disorder. When combined, these two facts effectively prove that depression and overthinking do not just have a cause-effect relationship. They feed and fuel one another continually and will keep doing so if you do not start working on your overthinking habit immediately.

Overthinking and Low Self-Esteem

Considering the relationship between overthinking and depression, it can be said that the ties that bind overthinking and self-esteem together run deeper than that. This is partly because depression can very quickly worsen a person's low self-esteem by increasing their feelings of worthlessness and guilt. If a person develops a depressive disorder, then their self-esteem will deteriorate further and add even more fuel to the fire of their overthinking. This will then keep fanning the flames of their depressive disorder, and before you know it, you will have yet another negative, cyclical relationship in your hands.

What if you engage in overthinking but are not depressed? Does that mean this habit of yours will have no bearing on your self-esteem? No, because self-esteem is not just related to depression, as you will remember. It is related to anxiety as well. That low self-esteem can lead to anxiety and fuel overthinking has already been established. People who have low self-esteem have this tendency to take how they feel about a particular situation—like a minor mistake they made, for instance—and use it to define how they feel in general (Arlin Cuncic, 2018). They develop entire beliefs about themselves and their relationships based on such things.

What does that mean in the context of relationship anxiety? Well, let's say you suffer from low self-esteem and you and your partner had a big fight. Let's also say that you suffer from low self-esteem. So, when the fight happens, your anxieties kick into high gear. You keep blaming yourself for the mistake you made. You conclude that your partner is going to dump you because of this, instead of, say, calming yourself down and logically thinking things through. These worries suddenly overtake your mind and you can neither put an end to them nor stop them. You become absolutely convinced that your relationship is in trouble and that you are a very bad person and partner. Meanwhile, your partner actually calms down and comes to you to make up. They apologize for their part in the fight, but that does not stop you from feeling guilty still. It also does not stop that little voice in your head that keeps saying that they are going to dump you soon.

Clearly, then, there is a tight relationship between anxiety, depression, and overthinking. The relationship between anxiety and these two mental health conditions is cyclical ones that are hard to break. Hard does not mean impossible though. Severing the connection between overthinking, anxiety, and depression is in fact more than possible. Not only is it possible, but it is absolutely necessary, that is if you want to lead a healthy relationship, look after your physical health and improve your mental well-being.

Key Takeaways

- Overthinking can be incredibly detrimental to both your mental and physical well-being.

- Excessive worrying and anxiety can manifest in your physical body as these are natural elements of human survival.

- Overthinking can lead to pervasive and disheartening thoughts, sapping away at your problem-solving abilities as well as the strength of your creativity.

- Anxiety and overthinking can have a devastating effect on one's self-esteem, often leading to feelings of worthlessness and guilt.

Chapter 3

Understanding Relationship Rumination

There is a rather extreme version of overthinking known as rumination and it can affect you and your relationship in a variety of negative ways. Rumination is the act of dwelling on negative feelings and the event that caused them—even when said events are rather minor—getting caught in repetitive thinking patterns (American Psychiatric Association, 2020). Rumination can easily lead to your developing an anxiety disorder or depressive disorder. It can also worsen any pre-existing condition you may have and chip away at your relationship over time.

What Is Rumination?

How bad can rumination really be, though? Well, rumination essentially causes your mind to become preoccupied with negative events and worsens your mood in the process. If you and your partner had a minor fight, for instance, rumination would make you dwell on it and amplify the negative feelings you experience as a result of that fight. This would make you perceive the fight in an even more negative light, making it appear worse than it was.

Unable to move on from the fight or the feelings it has generated, you would not be able to focus and rely on your problem-solving skills by, say, having a calm, constructive discussion with your partner. Instead, any conversation you tried to have would either devolve into another fight or you would become liable to avoid your partner, mired as you are in feelings of shame, guilt, and self-blame.

Being unable to resolve the argument would contribute to your negative feelings and you—and your partner, by extension—would thus become stuck in a very negative loop. So, how bad can rumination be? Bad enough to mess with your day-to-day and general mood, mindset, perception of reality, and even relationship, as you can see.

Scientists have discovered through various studies that rumination is the most common cause of depression and anxiety disorders (American Psychiatric Association, 2020). What makes rumination really difficult to stop is how fast it works. When you are ruminating, the thoughts that are running through your mind feel like they really *are* running and at lightning speed at that. The saying, "My mind is racing," would not be inaccurate to describe how rumination works (Sadurní Rodríguez, 2020). Temporary rumination can sometimes be normal, especially if you have experienced something unexpected and sudden, just as momentary stress and anxiety are perfectly normal. Most people engage in short-term rumination to analyze a problem at hand or gain some insight into it. Like anxiety and stress though, the problem begins when rumination turns into a constant habit.

It can be said there are two kinds of rumination then: the healthy and short-term one and the unhealthy and long-term one. Psychologists refer to the healthy kind of rumination as "reflection" and the unhealthy kind as "brooding" (Scott, 2019). One reason brooding is considered unhealthy is that worsens your mood and can lead to anxiety and depression, as you saw. Another is that it generates a feeling of helplessness in the person engaging in it. This helplessness is usually born of that person's inability to change a past event and how it transpired. If you are brooding over a fight you had with your partner, for instance, you find yourself thinking things like "I should have said XYZ instead." You might also start feeling helpless and hopeless because you can't go back in time to take back the things you said and say all these alternate responses you are thinking of now.

Brooding can be incredibly frustrating once you become aware of just how much time and energy you have spent on it. This can lead to a whole other bout of rumination, where you get angry at yourself for wasting so much of your energy on mentally rehashing a relatively small argument. Of course, then you will get angry at yourself for continuing to brood and get even more stuck in your negative thought patterns.

Why Do People Ruminate?

So, why do we do it? Why do we keep ruminating and brooding on things, even when we recognize how bad it is for us and our relationships? There are several root causes of rumination. One is the belief that by going over an occurrence, problem, or event, over and over again, we will be able to finally make sense of it. This is especially true for situations that we find difficult to accept and acknowledge. Left unchecked, this belief is actually what causes a person to switch from the good kind of rumination—reflection—to the bad kind—brooding.

Another reason why people ruminate is that they are seeking validation. Say, again, that you had an argument with your partner and you are sure you are right and they are wrong. The argument got quite heated and you got angry, frustrated, or upset. You might keep going over the argument in your mind, analyzing bits and pieces of it, so that you can say, "See! I was right!" Rumination, in this case, can become a toxic way of seeking the acknowledgment or validation you did not get from your partner. It can also be a way of trying to prove to yourself that you are right, even if you really are not, and of absolving yourself of responsibility. If the argument you had with your partner was about a mistake that you made, for instance, you might be brooding on it to find excuses as to why that mistake was not your fault.

Of course, there are certain characteristic factors that play a part in why people ruminate (Cirino, 2018). People who are perfectionists, for example, tend to be more inclined to ruminate and brood, especially if they make a mistake or something they've been working on turns out to be less than perfect. People who focus excessively on their relationships are generally more inclined to brood too. If your attention is focused mostly on picking apart your relationship and analyzing, then re-analyzing its minutiae, then it is only natural for you to start brooding when something goes wrong or even feels less than perfect, now is it not? This is especially true if you are in a relationship that is just not working. Having grown so used to prioritizing that relationship, you will be less likely to acknowledge that it is no longer working, after all, and far more likely to ruminate on it.

There are certain psychological reasons why people might ruminate too. Some people, for instance, care too much about what others think. This often causes them to constantly micromanage their own behavior and the way they express their thoughts. It even makes them edit their thoughts, opinions, and feelings before sharing them with others. When they make a mistake or when they get the feeling that the person opposite them, like their partner, such people end up brooding. They become consumed by what others are thinking about them and berate themselves for not saying or doing "the right thing" (Tartakovsky, 2015).

As you might have guessed, another culprit responsible for rumination habits and tendencies is low self-esteem. A person with low self-esteem is someone who is likely to blame themself for things that go wrong. If such a person goes through a breakup, for instance, instead of understanding that they split up because the two of them wanted inherently different things in life, they would blame themselves. They would probably think that their partner broke up with them because they are not good enough, or worthy of love. They would find some way of assigning blame to themselves and generalize by thinking that they could not make any of their relationships work. In doing so, they would be likely to start overthinking in their next relationship as well, effectively ensuring that it will fail.

Having said all that, it should be pointed out there are some biological reasons behind our rumination habits as well. There is a part of our brain that is known as the default mode network or DMN (Ma & Zhang, 2021). The DMN is made up of various, interconnected regions of the brain called the medial posterior cortex, medial prefrontal cortex (MPC), and bilateral inferior parietal lobule (IBL) (Sadurní Rodríguez, 2020). Brain scans taken with fMRI machines show that this part of the brain becomes activated when people start daydreaming and reminiscing, get lost in thought, or begin to ruminate.

When a person engages in one of these activities, their body goes into "auto-pilot" mode. DMN, then becomes active in this mode, when the individual is not actively paying attention to things like their surroundings or what they are doing. This activation is partly responsible for our tendency to ruminate and a key way of putting a stop to rumination is figuring out how to shut down DMN (Zhou et al., 2020).

This is one reason why distracting yourself with an activity that you have to pay attention to is an effective way of putting an end to rumination. Making yourself direct your attention actively to what you are doing, effectively takes you out of auto-pilot mode and switches off your DMN, but more on that later.

How Rumination Affects Relationships

Rumination can have a toxic effect on both you, as an individual, and your relationship. We've already seen that overthinking can cause you to do things like misinterpret your partner's motivations and behavior and sabotage your relationship. But the effects of rumination actually run deeper than that. They run so deep, in fact, that they can cause a healthy relationship to turn toxic.

One of the ways in which rumination turns a relationship toxic is by lowering your ability to regulate your emotions when you experience relationship struggles (Jostmann et al., 2011). That means that when you engage in rumination, two things happen at once:

- you become less able to manage and process negative emotions that arise as a result of a negative relationship event, such as an argument, disagreement, or your partner doing something that is hurtful for you (intentionally or not)

- you become less able to maintain your positive emotions about your relationship in general following a negative relationship event

These things cause your relationship to turn toxic or, alternatively, can cause it to fail, by keeping you from dealing with your emotions in a healthy way and forming an accurate perception of how your relationship is going. The negative feelings you are unable to regulate take over your reality completely, after all, and prevent you from being able to move past them. They keep coloring your understanding of your relationship in a negative light, even after the negative event that has made it arise has been resolved. If the negative feelings you were having trouble managing were the result of an argument, for instance, they might persist even after the fight is resolved. They might make you view everything your partner does thereafter in a negative way, which is bound to take its toll on you, your partner, and ultimately your relationship.

Rumination can further turn your relationship toxic because it can result in you and your partner engaging in a similar behavior known as co-rumination. Co-rumination happens when you and your partner start continually rehashing and rediscussing the same problem or problems without coming up with any type of solution. It is basically just stating the same negative things over and over again, the way you would in your mind, except with your partner (Kirmayer, 2018).

Instead of helping you come up with a compromise or solution and rather than helping you to communicate openly and effectively with your partner, this behavior causes the two of you to become stuck. Co-rumination between partners generates more and more negative feelings, the way regular rumination does. This, in turn, leads to even more co-rumination. For a lot of partners, then, co-rumination feels a lot like going round and round in a maze with no way out.

There are certain signs that indicate that you are overthinking things, as you will remember. Likewise, there are signs that you and your partner may be engaging in co-rumination. Without knowing what these signs are, confusing co-rumination with "sharing your feeling" becomes all too simple. Signs indicating that you and your partner are co-ruminating, then, are (American Psychological Association, 2023):

- Talking about the same, exact experiences, which evoke feelings of sadness, anger, envy, or jealousy in you, over and over again, with no change or resolution

- Not feeling like you have resolved or accomplished anything after you and your partner are done talking

- Always dwelling on negative feelings after talking about them with your partner

- An increase in depressive and anxiety-related symptoms after rehashing issues with your partner

The key thing to remember about rumination, whether you engage in co-rumination or not, is that it can poison a healthy relationship bit by bit, over time. In doing so, it can ultimately destroy that relationship. One way rumination does this is by keeping you from living in the present. If you are always stressed or worried about something that happened in the past or something that you fear will happen in the future, you can't very well enjoy the moment you are in (Times Entertainment Times, 2019). You can't really connect with your partner or make many meaningful memories either, which will only compound your negative feelings about your relationship.

Speaking of connecting, rumination can not only prevent you from deepening your bonds with your partner but also go so far as weakening them. By preventing you from regulating your emotions and keeping in tune with them, it'll make it impossible for you to communicate them to your partner. At the same time, this situation can hinder your ability to understand your partner's emotions and thoughts. Both these things are very necessary if you want to be able to form a deep connection with your partner.

The more your connection with your partner erodes as a result of rumination, overthinking, and relationship anxiety, the weaker your relationship will become. This situation will continue until the thread binding you and your partner becomes as thin as a single strand of hair, before snapping at last... That is if you don't take the necessary steps to end your rumination and overthinking habits once and for all.

Key Takeaways

- Rumination is the ultimate form of overthinking, and it can cause substantial harm to both an individual and their relationships.

- Unhelpful thoughts about negative events can quickly snowball, leading to a cycle of rumination that often results in depression or anxiety disorders.

- A variety of sources can spark rumination, such as a recurring issue in one's life, seeking validation from others, or underlying psychological aspects.

- Dwelling on the same thoughts and feelings can be damaging to your relationship because it may cause you and your partner to engage in co-rumination, a similar destructive pattern.

- When rumination, overthinking, and relationship anxiety start to erode your connection with your partner, the bond between you will undoubtedly become weaker.

Chapter 4

Importance of Self-Awareness in a Relationship

There are two kinds of rumination, as you now know: self-reflection and brooding. Self-reflection is a healthy kind of rumination. Self-reflection is the act of looking at your thoughts, feelings, behaviors, and motivations neutrally. The key word there is *neutrally* of course, and that is what makes self-reflection different from brooding and overthinking (Habash, 2022). Brooding and overthinking generate negative feelings about yourself and your relationship. Self-reflection does not. Instead, it allows you to see yourself as you are and your relationship as it truly is. It prevents you from becoming mired in negative thoughts and allows you to actually enjoy the moment that you are in.

The reason self-reflection allows you to do all this and more is that it is actually a practice of self-awareness, which is something that can help you to spot when you are overthinking and thus put a stop to it. It is something that can allow you to truly see and understand yourself and why you do the things you do. It can help you to better see the reality of your relationship and equip you with the tools you need to work on any relationship issues you may be having without becoming frustrated and hopeless. All of that, though, is contingent on your ability to practice your self-awareness. Luckily for everyone, self-awareness is not some ability like the perfect pitch that only a chosen few people are born with. Rather it is a skill that everyone inherently possesses and can develop over time.

What Is Self-Awareness?

Before diving deeper into how self-awareness can prevent overthinking, let's first properly understand what self-awareness is. To reiterate, self-awareness is your ability to unbiasedly understand your feelings, thoughts, actions, personality traits, values, and beliefs without making any kind of judgment about them. In essence, it is your ability to understand who you are as an individual. It is a state of being where you consciously bring your attention to your "self" (Cherry, 2020).

Since self-awareness is a state of being, it is not something that you can do 24/7. Your attention cannot be on your sense of self all of the time. If you want to practice self-awareness, then you have to do so periodically, by consciously bringing your attention to your "self" for bursts of time. When you are done, your attention will drift elsewhere, like the book you are reading, the work you have to do, or the friend you are talking to, for instance.

Practicing self-awareness like this is something that you learn to do over time, as scientists have observed. Human beings are not born completely self-aware, but they are all born with a nugget or shred of self-awareness within them. Babies, for instance, are born with the awareness that they are entirely separate, individual human beings from those around them. They differentiate between themselves and others through their sense of touch (Rochat, 2003). This is the first way self-awareness manifests in any human being. Later, their other senses become more pronounced and they begin to use them to differentiate between themselves and "others."

That shred of self-awareness that newborns have really started developing when they are about a year old. It becomes especially defined and pronounced when they are 18 months old. This is why 18-month-old babies try to touch their various body parts in the mirror when they are shown their own reflections. Their self-awareness allows them to recognize that those body parts belong to them and they reach out to touch that which belongs to them (Brooks-Gunn & Lewis, 1984). This only happens among babies that are over a year old though. Babies who are not yet one year old do not react in the same way, which indicates that their self-awareness is not developed enough for them to make that distinction at that point.

Scientists and psychologists believe that our self-awareness is governed by a region of the brain known as the cingulate cortex, which is found in the frontal lobe. The cingulate cortex is also a part of the DMS, as you will remember. Considering this, it can be said that it plays a part in both our ability to develop and practice self-awareness and our propensity for engaging in rumination.

As you may have gathered by now, your level of self-awareness keeps growing as you age. This process unfolds in five stages, the first of which is differentiation. Differentiation happens when babies recognize a person in the mirror, without really realizing who that person is (Rochat, 2003). The second stage is known as situation, where babies recognize themselves in the mirror. The third is identification, which is when their sense of self really starts settling, and the ideas of "I" and "me" form. The fourth permanence, where their self-awareness advances enough to allow them to identify themselves in photos and the like. The final stage is self-consciousness, which is when children start understanding that other people think of them and perceive them in different ways.

Once your self-awareness gets to the self-consciousness stage, one of two things can happen. Either you can keep developing it or you will not. Ideally, you want to develop your level of self-awareness. This is because being a self-aware individual has numerous benefits for you. Obviously, one benefit is that it keeps you from overthinking and ruminating on things and you will discover how it achieves this momentarily. For now, though, let's take a closer look at some of the other benefits self-awareness has to offer, which are that (Betz, 2021):

- it improves your decision-making skills.

- it increases your self-worth by allowing you to see both your strengths and your weaknesses.

- it improves your ability to communicate your feelings, thoughts, and needs better.

- it increases your ability to regulate both your positive and your negative emotions.

- it increases your ability to influence the outcome of events you have control over.

- it gives you the power to understand different perspectives and thus empathize more with others.

- it reduces your stress and anxiety levels by keeping you from becoming mired in negative thoughts and engaging in self-blame, which can evoke negative feelings like shame, embarrassment, anger, and pessimism.

- it helps you to maintain a more positive outlook, even when you are facing challenging situations, like having a major disagreement with your partner about an important matter.

- it enables you to put aside your biases, prejudices, and assumptions, which you might have otherwise been harboring without even realizing it.

- it helps you to strengthen all your relationships, including romantic ones

- it makes you live a happier life.

Why Self-Awareness Is Important in a Relationship

This might be unexpected to hear, but there are actually two different kinds of self-awareness: internal and external. Reaping these wonderful sounding benefits requires having both high levels of both internal self-awareness and external self-awareness (Eurich, 2018). Internal self-awareness is your understanding of things like your motivations, passions, and values, as well as your thoughts, feelings, and reactions. External self-awareness is your understanding of how others see you and what they think of you.

The reason you want your internal and external self-awareness levels to be high is that they create a sort of balance. If you have high levels of external awareness and low levels of internal awareness, then you likely will end up struggling to figure out your sense of identity. You will also constantly worry about how others see you because you will not be able to tell.

What if you have high levels of external self-awareness but low levels of internal awareness? In that case, you likely will become the type of person who acts a certain way but thinks and feels differently. You will have trouble expressing your real thoughts and feelings because you will worry you will not be liked or accepted by others. You will end up ignoring or dismissing your own needs in favor of meeting those of others. You will even do this in your relationships, including romantic ones. All that will lead to a lot of relationship issues and feed your overthinking habits, especially when your partner fails to anticipate your needs because you keep not sharing them. This will probably result in your relationship falling apart.

What if the situation is reversed? What if you have high levels of internal self-awareness but low levels of external awareness? While you will have a clear sense of who you are as a person in this case, you will probably refuse constructive feedback when others try to give it to you. You might even get defensive when people try to give you constructive feedback and interpret it as criticism or a kind of attack. This might cause you to lash out at your partner, say when they make a mild suggestion that sounds like a critique. That will obviously lead to arguments, especially if they happen often enough. At the same time, the mild critique you receive will activate your overthinking habits. You will end up turning that one suggestion into a massive issue that you keep coming back to again and again. That will not only destroy your peace of mind, but it can threaten to deal blows to your relationship too.

If you have high levels of internal and external self-awareness, though, you can avoid all of this. In this scenario, not only will you be fully aware of and at peace with who you are as a person, but you will be open and able to handle constructive criticism or feedback when it is given. You will be able to communicate your needs, wants, feelings, and thoughts to your partner freely and without issues. You will also be able to receive criticism and feedback without getting defensive or feeling attacked. What's more, you will be able to do all this without either of these things kicking your overthinking tendencies into overdrive.

Now that we know why having high levels of self-awareness is important, let's take a look at what self-awareness can really do for your relationship. The key to maintaining a healthy relationship—be it a romantic one or some other kind of relationship—is to cultivate a strong sense of self-awareness.

One reason for this is that self-awareness helps you develop your empathic abilities. Empathy is your ability to put yourself in someone else's shoes. It is your ability to understand how other people are feeling. This is something that you can't even begin to do, though, if you can't understand yourself. This is why studies show that people who are highly empathic, meaning very good at understanding other people's feelings, are also very good at understanding their own feelings (Newman, 2018). One study that tried to measure the relationship between empathy and self-awareness found that of its 700 participants, those who proved to be self-aware also tended to have higher levels of cognitive empathy—meaning they were able to understand other people's perspectives and emotions better—and of affective empathy—meaning they were better able to respond to other people's emotions.

Empathy is understandably vital for maintaining a healthy relationship. When you develop your empathic abilities, you improve your ability to truly understand and respond to your partner's feelings and perspectives. Rather than try and guess their motives or, worse, ascribe motives to them, you become able to comprehend what theirs really are. This helps reduce your overthinking habits significantly, seeing as a lot of people overthink and ruminate, trying to understand why their partners did or said something. The less we engage in overthinking, the more we can communicate our feelings, thoughts, and needs to our partners, rather than bury them. The more you openly communicate the better your relationship with your partner, and the healthier and stronger your relationship will be.

The reason self-awareness and empathy have such a direct relationship is that self-awareness turns down the volume of the voices crowding your mind or does away with them entirely. By toning down your overthinking habits, it makes room for your understanding of other people. In short, it gives you the space you need to truly connect with others. This simply is not something you can do without developing a thorough awareness and understanding of yourself though. After all, how can you even begin to understand other people, if you have no idea what you yourself are feeling, thinking, or believing in, to begin with?

Another key reason why self-awareness ends up being very good for relationships is that they help you to show up as your best self. That does not mean hiding your perceived faults, mistakes, or weaknesses. Rather it means recognizing them, fully accepting yourself as you are, and, at the same time, being willing to proactively work on those weaknesses. Say that you were really poor at time management. As a result, you keep being late to dates and events with the person you are in a relationship with, even when you make plans well in advance. Let's also say that your levels of internal and external self-awareness are fairly low. So, when your partner tries to talk to you about this issue, your insecurities kick in. You get defensive, make excuses, and the conversation devolves into a massive fight. Afterward, you replay the fight in your mind over and over and over again. On the one hand, you keep trying to justify your behavior. On the other hand, you keep worrying that your partner is going to leave you. Before you know it, you have spent several days, semi-sleepless nights included, going over the same things and the same what-ifs with no discernible result.

What if you practiced self-awareness though? How might things go then? Well, in that case, you might respond wholly differently to your partner when they talk to you about this behavior that bothers them. You might listen to them openly and without getting defensive. You might accept the constructive criticism they give you and resolve to work on it, rather than makeup excuses. After the conversation, you might think about it for a period of time, but then you would be able to focus on other things. You would not replay what happened again and again and you probably would not lose any sleep over it. The following day, you would talk to your partner the way you normally would, since you did not have an argument in the first place.

Last but not least, by practicing self-awareness, you would be happier both in your relationship and with yourself. This would stem from your ability to accept yourself, faults and shortcomings, and all. Again, accepting these would not mean saying "This is just how I am," and moving on. It simply means being able to acknowledge that you have such weaknesses, work on them actively and without judging or berating yourself, and grow as an individual human being. Your ability to accept yourself would thus be directly proportional to your overall happiness.

Practicing Self-Awareness in a Relationship

So, do you know what self-awareness is and why it is so important? How can you go about "practicing" self-awareness? While we will be exploring some of these techniques in greater detail in a later chapter, let's take a quick look at some of them now. One great way of doing this is keeping a journal. Journaling has long been hailed as a great method of self-reflection and self-awareness (de Dios González., 2022). It is an activity that is great for processing and resolving whatever doubts you may be experiencing, understanding and regulating your own emotion, and connecting with yourself. At the same time, it can be a great tool for resolving any conflicts you may be having with others, such as your partner. This is because journaling gives you the distance you need to look at conflicts, arguments, and other such events from afar. It can help you to better comprehend other people's thoughts, points of view, feelings, motivations, and reactions. In other words, it can be a practice of both self-awareness and empathy, which as we know are connected to one another. At its core, journaling can help you identify key issues and problems and find solutions that would actually work.

The great thing about journaling is that you don't need to write a masterpiece when writing a journal entry. All you need to do is write honestly and regularly. That does not mean you have to write every day. Sometimes life gets a little too hectic for that to be a possibility and that is understandable. But you should try to journal a couple of times a week, at the very least. One thing that could help you to stick to a schedule is trying to write around the same time every couple of days or so. If you work a 9-to-5 job, for instance, maybe you could write in your journal around 7 p.m. regularly. If you are less busy in the mornings than in the afternoons or at night, then perhaps 10 a.m. might be a good time to take pen to paper for you.

Once you sit down to journal, remember to explore your feelings and thoughts openly and honestly. The key word there is "explore." That means you should not just write what you are feeling or how you might have reacted to a specific event or trigger that day. You should also make a conscious effort to understand the reasons behind it. As you are writing, don't try to rationalize your decision, reactions, or actions. Rationalization is not exploration and it is the latter you want to focus on if you truly want to understand yourself. While you are doing that, make sure you don't put too much pressure on yourself to write a certain way. A journal entry does not have to be perfect, after all. No one is going to grade you on it. It does not matter if there are numerous grammatical errors in it. What matters is that you make a genuine effort to understand yourself and the rest will come.

Another great way of practicing and improving your self-awareness is meditation and mindfulness practices. The thing about meditation and mindfulness is that they both are processes that help you to see yourself better. In that sense, engaging in them is akin to wiping a thick coat of dust off the surface of a mirror.

According to one study, such practices actually decrease the activity that is observed in brain regions, meaning for instance the prefrontal cortical midline structures, that correlate to rumination and overthinking (Lutz et al., 2016). At least according to brain scans taken of people who regularly meditate, don't meditate at all, and who haven't meditated before but started to for the purposes of the study.

Meditation and mindfulness are all about observing yourself—and everything you are thinking and feeling—without judging or criticizing yourself for them. They are about allowing you to experience a feeling or emotion, sitting with it for a while, and letting it drift away on its own. When you engage in meditation, the areas of the brain that drive rumination quiet down. At the same time, the areas of the brain that control or are related to your ability to perceive yourself and others become more active (Dolan, 2017). It can be said, then, that practicing mindfulness meditation can help you strengthen the regions of your brain associated with awareness while weakening the ones controlling your rumination tendencies. It can effectively help you grow as an individual, improve your relationship, and silence overthinking, one day at a time.

These days, there are nearly countless meditation and mindfulness apps you can try out and take advantage of. There are also various classes you can take, books you can read, videos you can watch, podcasts you can listen to, and more. Now it might be that you find meditation to be a rather challenging practice. You might find yourself getting impatient or restless while trying to meditate. You might also have trouble keeping your mind in the present moment and not following after whatever negative thoughts pop into your mind. If that is the case for you, then keep your initial meditation sessions only a minute long. It should not be all that hard to sit still for a minute and focus on things like your breathing, should it? After a while, you can start extending your meditation time, but you should do so bit by bit.

One final method you can use to increase your self-awareness is to ask for and receive constructive feedback from others. Before you do this, you should remind yourself that feedback and criticism are two inherently different things. Criticism is something that is negative and that seems to be about something that you cannot change. It is something that aims to keep you down, rather than help you to grow. Constructive feedback, on the other hand, is something that can help you to accept your weaknesses without judgment, figure out what you need to work on, and improve upon yourself with self-awareness.

The problem with constructive feedback is that a lot of people confuse it with criticism and respond to it as though it were. When this happens, your brain's defensive mechanism kicks in and causes you to see feedback as a threat (Admin, 2016). This is simply how our brain works in a biological and neurological method. That does not mean, however, that we can't take this kind of response, which the brain gives, out of effect. We absolutely can by asking others to give us constructive feedback and using certain grounding, and neurological techniques to react differently than how our brains want to react to it. Labeling the emotions that you feel when you are receiving feedback is one such technique. This is a technique that works because when you label or name an emotion you are feeling, you reduce the activity levels occurring in your amygdala. Your amygdala is the part of your brain that is in charge of managing emotions, including fear, which kicks into gear when you sense a threat. When you name an emotion, you basically take your brain's attention from the amygdala and direct it to other regions of your brain. Hence the lowered level of activity. This essentially decreases the amount of fear you feel, which in turn makes it easier for you to receive feedback.

Another neurological, grounding technique you can use when getting feedback from your partner is to reanalyze the situation you are in. Psychologists refer to this technique as cognitive reappraisal. It is known to be very effective because it makes you consciously shift your perspective about the process of receiving feedback. Put simply, it makes you go from "the glass is half empty" to "the glass is half full." Both are accurate statements, of course, but the emotions they evoke in you are completely different, are they not?

Granted, both labeling and cognitive reappraisal are challenging skills. Mastering them takes a lot of practice. However, the more you try to do them, the more you will be able to. The more you do them, the easier these practices will become and the more they will raise your level of self-awareness. After a certain point, you will find that you don't have to make any conscious effort to use these skills. They will have become reflexes for you, so will have self-awareness and self-reflection. Overthinking and rumination, meanwhile, will have fallen to the wayside and become less able to inflict damage on you and your relationship.

Key Takeaways

- Self-awareness means having the capacity to confidently understand your motivations, behaviors, emotions, and values without attaching any kind of moral opinion or personal assessment.

- Developing an internal self-awareness enables you to comprehend your motivations, desires, and beliefs.

- External self-awareness gives you insight into the perceptions of others; their views of who you are and how they experience interacting with you.

- To become a well-rounded individual, it is important to develop both aspects in tandem.

- Cultivating a deep understanding of oneself is the secret ingredient to sustaining any type of relationship—romantic, professional, or otherwise.

- Developing self-awareness comes with an arsenal of techniques that can help you to address any issues or disagreements between yourself and your partner.

Chapter 5

Strategies for Overcoming Overthinking in Relationships

Preventing overthinking in relationships requires a four-pronged approach: nurturing positivity, implementing mindfulness, practicing clear communication, and reconnecting with your values. What do those mean? Nurturing positivity means maintaining a positive mindset. This does not mean wearing rose-tinted glasses that skew your perception of things, of course. Rather, it means being optimistic and allowing positive thoughts and emotions to fuel you. Overthinking, as you will recall, feeds off of negative emotions and thoughts, not positive ones. Mindfulness, meanwhile, is the act of intentionally and consciously bringing your attention to the present moment you are living through, rather than being dragged to the past by rehashing past events or the future by concocting various what-if scenarios. Clear communication is the ability to clearly and effectively communicate your needs, wants, emotions, and thoughts to other people, such as your partner. Finally, reconnecting with your values entails truly understanding what your values are and taking actions that embody and reflect them.

So, how exactly can these skills help you to put an end to overthinking? How can they prevent overthinking and rumination from affecting your relationship? What strategies can you use to develop and make use of these skills? To uncover all this, we'll have to take a much closer look at each and every one of these abilities.

Nurturing Positivity

A positive mindset is a kind of mental attitude that allows you to focus on the bright side of things (Ackerman, 2018). It is an attitude that helps you remain optimistic in various situations and conditions. For instance, if you were to go through a breakup or suffer a setback at work, your positive attitude would help you to get through it. A positive attitude, though, does not mean ignoring the negative or challenging things that happen in your life or the negative feelings that they evoke. We have feelings for a reason, after all, and should allow ourselves to feel them, including the negative ones. A positive mindset allows you to do that while also enabling you to make the best of the circumstances you have to work with. In doing so, it increases your level of resilience, as well as your creative problem-solving capabilities.

A positive mindset has six defining characteristics. Think of these as signs that you have a positive mindset, which can be summed up as (Ackerman, 2018):

- optimism
- resilience
- acceptance
- integrity
- mindfulness
- gratitude

The more you are able to cultivate it, the more obvious these signs will become. The first of these signs, optimism, means being able to look on the bright side of this, as you know. But it also means being willing to take a chance on things, like a new relationship, for instance, despite knowing you might fail, rather than assuming the worst. Given that, optimism is both a quality that makes you braver and one that is less prone to overthinking. After all, someone who is able to take a chance on things, will not keep thinking "I wish I had tried to work things out with my ex," over and over again. Instead, they already would have taken the leap.

Next, there is resilience. Resilience is your ability to bounce back from challenges, disappointments, apparent failures, and generally recover from the blows that life may deal you. If your partner gets a sudden job offer that forces them to move away and results in the two of you trying out a long-distance relationship, for example, your resilience will be what keeps you going. It will be what keeps you from asking, "Can we really do this?" and more optimistic even while taking on the challenges of this new relationship format.

Acceptance, as we have seen, is a very significant part of self-awareness. It stands to reason then, that it is equally as big a part of maintaining a positive mindset. After all, it is that which allows you to accept your faults, mistakes, and failures and grow from them. It is what gives you the ability to say, "I am not this one mistake," and the focus on how you can improve yourself, rather than continually replay that mistake in your mind.

Your integrity is essentially the state of being honest and honorable. It is being able to develop a value system and live in accordance with it. This is something only people with high levels of self-awareness are able to do. It keeps you from behaving in a way that would not fit in with your morals and values, such as cheating for instance. In doing so, it keeps you from ruminating on that behavior, thereby adding to the feelings of shame, guilt, or anger for having done things that you don't really believe in.

Like acceptance, mindfulness is deeply connected to self-awareness as well. It gives you the power to understand yourself, which in turn makes communicating aspects of yourself to your partner possible. Simultaneously, it allows you to develop your empathic abilities, thereby permitting you to understand and connect with other people, such as your partner, better.

Finally, gratitude is a state of actively appreciating the good things in your life, even or, maybe, especially when things get challenging and tough. Gratitude can be a great tool, in and of itself, for refocusing your attention and mentality in such circumstances. If you are having relationship troubles, for instance, and get caught in overthinking loops where you are continually questioning whether your relationship will work or not, gratitude can come to your aid. It can help you to remember and focus on the good parts of your relationship, the parts to be grateful for, and keep your mind from being overtaken by the more negative ones. It can help you to maintain a more balanced understanding of your relationship and cut your overthinking and rumination habits off at the knees.

The characteristics that make up a positive mindset provide you with the toolkit you need to handle different circumstances and the negative thoughts and emotions they may spark. They can keep you from wallowing in negative emotions and past mistakes, but they can only do so if you actively work to develop and maintain a positive mindset. One phenomenal way of doing this is using positive affirmations. That may sound like a hippie-esque bit of advice straight out of Instagram, but the thing is, affirmations actually work on a scientific and neurological level.

Positive affirmations are statements or phrases you repeat to yourself on a regular, ideally daily, basis to challenge negative thoughts. Remember those negative thoughts that run on a loop in your mind when you are overthinking? Well, affirmations are the exact opposite of them. That is why they can be really great remedies for them. For that to work, you will have to start your day with positive affirmations. You can also consciously pull out your affirmations any time you catch yourself becoming swept away by your negative thoughts, and then start repeating them. You would be surprised as to how quickly affirmations can put an end to overthinking in this way.

Positive self-affirmations work because your brain, more specifically your subconscious, cannot actually tell the difference between what's real and what's imaginary (Raypole, 2020). Let me explain. When you repeat a self-affirmation, such as "I am worthy of being loved," you create a mental image in your mind of a version of you that is worthy of being loved. Your conscious mind knows that this image is not real, it is one you have created. Your unconscious mind, however, does not realize this, because, again, it can't tell the difference between the "real" and the "imaginary." So, it reacts to that image as though it were real. This generates positive thoughts and positive emotions in you. It also primes your behavior, so that you act in a way that a person who is worthy of love would act (MalPaper, 2021).

Your unconscious mind's inability to distinguish between reality and imaginary also plays an important part in overthinking, in that it can make it worse. If you find yourself swept away by worries that your partner will cheat on you, for example, and keep concocting scenarios of walking in on them while they are cheating on you, then your subconscious mind will not be able to tell that that image is not real. Instead, it'll react as though it were real, which will trigger all kinds of negative emotions in you like anger, disappointment, heartbeat, anxiety, worry, and grief, as though your relationship were already over. This will happen every time you overthink or ruminate in this way and each instance will prime your behavior toward your partner, thus driving a wedge between you two.

You can avoid this, though, by countering thoughts and scenarios like this with self-affirmations. In doing so, you can get your unconscious mind to believe what you want it to believe and change your attitude, increase your positivity, and prime your behavior. It must be noted though that self-affirmations need to be followed by actions for them to work. Words that are not followed by actions can only take you so far. Your self-affirmations, then, can be considered a first step in your journey to stop overthinking and make decisions born out of positive feelings, rather than negative ones exacerbated by overthinking.

If you are still skeptical about whether self-affirmations really work, you will be relieved to hear that there is even more scientific evidence indicating that they do. Some years ago, a study was conducted where MRI scans of various individuals were taken. These scans showed that certain brain regions of people lit up after they practiced self-affirmations. This meant that those regions became more active. One region that became more active was the ventromedial prefrontal cortex, which, aside from being a mouthful, is responsible for your ability to process information about yourself and assign positive values and beliefs to yourself (Cascio et al., 2015).

Given all these facts, it can be safely said that self-affirmations work. Ultimately, they both increase your positive mindset and reduce your negative thoughts. The best thing about self-affirmations is that they are very easy to practice. You can find any number of them on social media, online, or in various articles and videos. You can also come up with unique affirmations that are just for you. If you are going to do this, one thing you should do is to make sure that your affirmations are realistic. If they are not, you will not be able to follow through with the actions that they require, no matter how hard you try. This will have the opposite effect of what you want, in that it will damage your positive mindset and worsen your overthinking habits, by causing you to latch onto thoughts like, "I knew I could not do it," or "I'm never going to get this right." If your self-affirmations are realistic, though, the actions associated with them will be very doable, and enacting them will only strengthen your positive mindset.

Another great activity for nurturing a positive mindset is to actively work on transforming your negative self-talk into positive self-talk. Everyone has a running dialogue in their minds, where they narrate events and beliefs to themselves and respond to them. In this regard, self-talk is a bit like the voice-over of a movie or TV show where you are the main character. There are two different kinds of self-talk: positive and negative. Positive self-talk is the kind of inner dialogue where you talk positively to and about yourself. Negative self-talk is the exact opposite of that. The former can be uplifting and motivating. The latter can get you down and add gasoline to the fire of your overthinking habits (Mead, 2019).

Both positive and negative self-talk are effective in determining your attitude, feelings, mood, and, therefore, behavior in a relationship. They are able to do this for the same reason that self-affirmations work: They present your brain with a kind of image of yourself, which your unconscious mind then takes as an undeniable reality. Positive self-talk can be incredibly effective in reducing overthinking and achieving things you want to achieve. This is why athletes use it really, very frequently. Michael Jordan, for instance, used to envision his victories before games and engage heavily in positive self-talk before games. In doing so, he would motivate himself, increase his belief in himself and his abilities, and usually the best performance he possibly could give on the court (Hehir, 2020).

Self-talk is a practice and phenomenon that scientists have studied at length. Their findings ultimately confirmed how effective it is. According to one study conducted with professional athletes, for instance, it was discovered that those athletes who engaged more in negative self-talk, where they expressed things like fear of failure and performance anxiety, for instance, tended to play worse games and make more mistakes. The athletes who engaged in positive self-talk, on the other hand, tended to perform much better in their chosen field of sports, win more victories, make fewer mistakes, and even bounce back more quickly from failures and mistakes (Mead, 2019). Just as Michael Jordan used to.

Positive self-talk comes with a myriad of benefits, the most obvious of which is that it reduces overthinking and cultivates a positive mindset. At the same time, it increases your confidence levels, which is important because we know that low confidence and self-esteem are the root causes of relationship anxiety and overthinking. It even helps to reduce your stress and anxiety levels, which, again, can stoke up rumination patterns. This is because positive self-talk contributes to a positive mindset and makes people more optimistic. The more optimistic a person is, the more they become able to turn to healthy coping mechanisms to manage stress and anxiety, or so studies show (Iwanaga et al., 2004). The more they manage stress and anxiety in a healthy way, the less likely they will be to get swept away by negative thoughts. Instead, they will just be able to process them using their coping mechanisms.

A final, proven benefit of positive self-talk is that it can help you build better, stronger relationships (Mead, 2019). This is because positive self-talk increases your self-acceptance, self-confidence, and self-esteem levels. People who exhibit higher levels of these things are able to connect with others with fewer doubts and hesitancies. They don't worry about being liked or judged by them or at least they don't worry about it as much. Instead, they let themselves be who they are with, say, their partners, and allow them to get closer. This of course deepens their emotional connection with their partners, which further increases the positive emotions that they are feeling.

If you want to practice positive self-talk, you will have to make a conscious effort to do so. That means recognizing when you are engaging in negative self-talk, like when you are overthinking, hitting pause for a moment, and actively trying to transform that bit of negative self-talk into a positive or at least neutral version of it. This requires some degree of self-awareness; something you can do more of, now that you know how. Once you have identified negative self-talk, your first task will be to label it. This is because labeling negative thoughts effectively depower the part of your brain that activates when you are generating them, as you may remember. There are four different categories of negative self-talk and labeling the thought you are having means naming which category it falls into.

The four categories of negative self-talk are:

- catastrophizing
- polarizing
- personalizing
- magnifying

To take a closer look at these categories, **catastrophizing** means assuming the worst of a given situation. A good example of this would be thinking, "My partner is going to dump me," after you have had an argument. **Polarizing** means seeing things in black and white, bad and good. It means leaving no gray areas in which to operate. **Personalizing**, on the other hand, is blaming yourself when something goes wrong, even if you are not responsible for it in any way, shape, or form. Finally, **magnifying** is dismissing the good that exists in a given situation or event and focusing only on the bad. If you are having relationship issues, for instance, and dismiss all the good parts of your relationship, like they don't matter, choosing to focus solely on the bad, you are very obviously magnifying.

So, you have caught yourself overthinking and engaging in negative self-talk. You have labeled that thought and labeled it as catastrophizing, let's say. What do you do now? Well, now, you have to question that thought. Start by asking yourself whether this thought is positive or negative, constructive or destructive. Answer the question honestly, then ask yourself what you would say to your partner, the person you love if they expressed this exact thought. Again, be honest with yourself. Once you have settled on what answer you would give to your partner, use it to rewrite the negative self-talk in a more positive way. If the thought you had was, "My partner is not picking up their phone. What if they are cheating on me?"; for example, then you can replace it with something like "There are any number of reasons why my partner might not be able to pick up the phone right now. They will respond to me when they are able to."

Replacing negative self-talk with positive self-talk like this will be a challenge at first. But as with anything, the more you practice it, the more you will be able to do it. A great way to practice this skill more is to get a notebook and write down your negative thoughts on one page. Then you can write down their positive versions directly opposite, and repeat them to yourself. If you wrote, "I will never be able to make this relationship work," in the negative column for instance, you can write, "We might be facing some issues right now, but we can work through them together," or "I can make this relationship work, so long as I keep communicating openly and honestly with my partner." As you write, you will likely be surprised to see just how often you engage in negative self-talk, at least at first. After a while though, you will realize that you have been engaging in this practice less and less. You will also realize that you feel more optimistic and confident these days. All because you took the time you needed to look over your thoughts with a non-judgmental eye and put in a little bit of work to give them a more positive spin.

Implementing Mindfulness

We've already explored mindfulness a bit in the previous chapter and know how effective it can be in increasing our self-awareness. But what does it have to do with maintaining a positive mindset? Plenty because mindfulness is one of its central tenets. An important reason for this is that mindfulness helps you to understand your emotions and thoughts fully, thereby promoting your emotional well-being (Ackerman, 2019). This is due to the fact that mindfulness allows you to observe your thoughts and emotions without judging them. This helps you to practice self-acceptance and utilize important techniques for changing your negative thoughts into positive ones, like positive self-talk, as we just learned. It also allows you to turn to healthy coping mechanisms when you catch yourself becoming stressed or anxious, thus preventing such feelings from triggering rumination and overthinking.

All of this, though, is contingent on your ability to practice mindfulness, though. There are numerous ways of practicing mindfulness and mindfulness meditation is one of them. However, seeing as meditation will be covered at length in a later chapter and has already been explored to some degree in a previous one, let's take a closer look at other mindfulness techniques you can try out.

Since mindfulness is all about awareness and self-awareness, you can get into the habit of practicing it using the raisin exercise (Ackerman, 2017). This exercise, which actually requires you to get a packet of raisins, is a great technique for you to try, especially if you are unused to working on your awareness and mindfulness levels. It is also great for those individuals who struggle with staying in the present moment. The way it works is this: you pour the raisin you bought into a bowl, close your eyes, and dig your hand into it. Try to pay close attention to how the raisins feel around your hand, inside your palm, and against your skin. Take a handful of them out of the ball, and focus on the feel of them in your hand. What does their texture feel like? Take them up toward your nose. What do they smell like? Pop a few into your mouth. What do they taste like and how would you describe their texture upon your tongue, against your teeth? Play with the raisins left in your hand and try to really feel how their skin can be manipulated through your touch.

The reason this exercise is a great way of getting into mindfulness practices is that it makes you pay attention to sensory details that you normally would overlook. It makes you actively notice everything there is to notice about the raisins in your hand. In doing so, it trains your mind to focus on the sensations that you would feel at a given moment, rather than on the running thoughts in your head, be they about the past or the future.

There is a (little) more complicated version of this exercise known as the body scan. It essentially achieves the same thing that the raisin experiments do, by training your mind to pay attention to the sensations your body experiences in the present moment. The difference here is that the object that you direct your attention to is not something external, like the raisin. Instead, it is your very body. To do the body scan, you must first sit down comfortably, or lie down on a comfortable surface, like a bed. Once you are in position, you must take care to lie as still as you can. You start the practice by taking a deep breath and actively directing your attention to that breath. How does it feel going in through your nostrils? How does the air feel traveling through to your lungs? What does the sensation of your lungs inflating feel like? What's the rhythm of your breathing? Is it slow? Is it fast? Does it keep changing up or is it fairly steady? Ideally, you want to keep your breathing rhythm steady as you focus on it and should not deliver your attention from it until it has settled into a regular pace.

Once your breathing has settled into a slow, deep rhythm, move your attention to the tip of your toes, a part of your body you normally don't pay any mind to, unless you stub your toe. Really try to feel how your toes feel. Are they pressed up against the ground? If so, how does the ground beneath your toes feel? Are you wearing socks? If so, how does the fabric feel against them? Are your toes hot at the moment or are they cold?

Move your attention away from your toes, slowly and gently, and focus on your feet in this manner next. Then have your focus trickle up to your ankles, calves, knees, and up your body, as though your attention were a body of water you were slowly submerging yourself in. Keep going, without rushing, until you get to the very crown of your head.

Exercises like these can go a long way to increasing your mindfulness and, subsequently, your awareness levels. Higher mindfulness and awareness levels translate to more positive emotions and thoughts. This is because they give you the ability to notice the positive parts of your life and relationships a great deal more than you otherwise could have (Lindsay et al., 2018). Thus they support a positive mindset and cut off the source that rumination feeds off of.

Practicing Clear Communication

Being unable or unwilling to clearly communicate your thoughts, feelings, and needs to your partner causes you to start overthinking, as we said. Keeping things in like this can make you replay the things you should have said to your partner and berate yourself for not saying them. Alternatively, it can make you get angry at your partner for not being able to guess or divine the thoughts, feelings, and needs that you haven't been sharing with them. Practicing your clear communication skills can put an end to all of that. Communicating things like your feelings and needs can ensure that they are met. They can make you feel that you are heard and that your opinions and emotions matter. It can enable your partner to respond to you in the way that you need, which can make you feel loved and cherished. Understandably, all of this can and does contribute to your cultivating and maintaining a positive mindset.

Being able to communicate clearly with other people such as your partner requires knowing what clear communication is and what it is not. Clear communication, for instance, does not mean blurting everything that comes to your mind the moment that it does. It also does not mean verbally attacking the person before you. What exactly is clear and positive communication then and how can you do it?

Despite what you might think, clear, positive communication does not mean not sharing your negative thoughts and emotions. It certainly does not mean keeping things that bother you to yourself. Rather it means communicating all these things and more in a constructive and easily understandable manner. This is, let's be honest, easier said than done, especially if your emotions are running high. Yet, it is not impossible to do.

The first rule to communicating clearly and positively with your partner is to always use "I statements." This is especially true when you are having a disagreement or even a full-blown argument. It is true when you are trying to tell your partner that they did upset or hurt you, even if they did not realize it at the time. I statements are phrases that begin with things like (Better Health, 2014):

- I feel...

- I need...

- I want...

If you are trying to tell your partner that something they did hurt you for instance, you can say something like, "I feel like I'm being ignored when you cut me off in the middle of a sentence," or "I feel lonely when you go out with your work friends every night." Such statements can be very effective for two reasons. The first is that they don't assign blame to their partner, which phrases like, "You keep silencing me when you cut me off," or "You value spending time with your work friends more than you value spending time with me," do. The second benefit of "I statements" is that they communicate your feelings, and by extension your needs depending on what you are saying, very clearly to your partner. These two things change how your partner reacts to what you are saying. The first has them consider their behavior and your feelings. It has them recognize areas of change so that they can give you what you need. The second puts them on the defensive by making them feel attacked or criticized. This makes them more likely to launch a counterattack, start yelling, and accuse you of various things. As you might have guessed, this is a situation that can devolve into major arguments that would lead you to bouts of overthinking, very, very quickly.

Of course, using "I statements" is not the only rule you should follow if you want to communicate clearly with your partner. You should also focus on being as clear as you possibly can be. This might be difficult to do in the heat of the moment. If that is the case, taking a breath and thinking through what it is you want and need to say would be a good idea. In fact, thinking through the things you want to communicate to your partner is always a good idea. If you want to discuss a relationship issue, a need you have, or something that is important to you, you should set aside some time beforehand to go over it in your mind. You should ask yourself what it is you want to say. What message do you really want to communicate? What do you want your partner to know or understand once your conversation is over? Once you have nailed that down, ask yourself what the best way of explaining and relaying that is. If it helps, try journaling about this to gain clarity on your message yourself.

Once you know what it is you truly want to say, reach out to your partner and set aside some time to talk things through. This way, you can avoid having to squeeze an important conversation in between a million to-dos and thus rushing through things. Remember that rushing through important conversations can lead to a lot of miscommunication and misunderstandings, which is why you want to avoid them. Miscommunication and misunderstandings can go both ways though. This is why it is important that you listen to your partner actively. Tell them what you need to tell them, using I statements, and then allow them a chance to speak. Let them communicate their own perspective, reasoning, emotions, reactions, and thoughts. Try to be empathetic as you listen to them and ask clarifying questions, such as, "So, you are saying that ... Did I understand that correctly?" This way, you can make sure that you understand your partner correctly and demonstrate that you are paying attention. This is something that can both create greater understanding between you and your partner and make them feel that they are being heard.

The positive emotions this will invoke in them will typically make them emulate your behavior. In other words, observing your active listening skills in action can make your partner start practicing them as well. When you practice clear communication, then, you lead by example, in a sense, and have your partner start doing the same as well. All this reinforces the positive feelings you have about yourselves, one another, and your relationship. It is no wonder, then, that clear, positive communication can do wonders for your relationship, while turning down the volume of the negative thoughts in your head.

Reconnecting with Your Values

The last element of positive thinking is reconnecting with your values. Your values can be summed up as the core beliefs that give your life direction and give you meaning. They can only do so, though, if you listen to them and understand them fully. When you don't understand your values, you become unable to understand why you think, behave, feel, and even believe in the things that you do. At least on a conscious level. Your subconscious mind, however, remains aware of your values. So, when you do something that goes against your values, you recognize that. You feel things like shame, anger toward yourself, and embarrassment, without fully being able to explain why. If you were to lie to your partner, for instance, and lying runs counter to your values, this can cause your negative thoughts to spiral in all sorts of directions.

You might keep getting angry at yourself for lying, while questioning why you felt the need to do so, without being able to come up with an answer for it. You might keep trying to justify your behavior, over and over again. You might stress that your partner will discover that you lied. Whatever the case may be, you will ultimately find yourself ruminating in a bad mood and caught in a negative mindset, that will further damage your relationship down the line.

The simplest way to avoid all this is to connect with your values, of course, and work on identifying them. The process of identifying your values starts with asking yourself certain questions, like (Mind Tools Content Team, n.d.):

- When am I at my happiest? What am I doing when I am happy? What truly brings me joy?

- What makes me the proudest? Why does this thing fill me with pride? What factors contribute to my feeling this way?

- When was the last time I felt fully satisfied? What was I doing at that time? Why did that action or event cause me satisfaction?

A great trick for exploring the answer to these questions in depth is to do so in writing. Your journal might be a great place for doing so. Once you have answered all these questions, you should take a close look at them to see what values they correspond with the most. Is it honesty? Commitment? Cooperation? Is it something else entirely? As you are considering these, write all the values that seem to correspond with your answers on a page. For now, don't worry about how many values you are writing. All that matters is that you get them out onto the page. When you are finished, though, go over the entire list and ask yourself, "Which five values are most important to me out of this entire list?"

A good way of narrowing down your values list to your top five is to take them one pair at a time and ask yourself which would you choose over the other. Which of those two values is more important for you? By going through your list like this, you can narrow it down bit by bit, until you are left with those five options. Once you have them in hand, you can question them one last time, by asking yourself whether they make you feel good or not. You can also ask if acting on these values would make you feel proud of yourself.

If the answer to those questions is "yes," then there is only one thing left for you to do and that is to figure out what kinds of behavior correspond to your top values. This is not something you should do just one time and then move on from. It is something that you should keep in the back of your mind when making decisions. This way you can be sure that the actions you take or don't take always align with your values and never go against them. By keeping your values and your behavior consistent with one another, you can prevent a great deal of overthinking, and keep from perpetuating the kind of negative mindset that would lead to it. You can make sure you maintain a healthy relationship in the process, unmarred by actions that go against your values and the rumination that would lead.

Key Takeaways

- If you're looking to protect your relationship from overthinking, consider a four-step approach: foster positivity, exercise mindfulness techniques, engage in open dialogue with each other and reaffirm the values that matter most.

- A positive mindset gives you the necessary skills and abilities to navigate tricky situations, along with any negative feelings they might bring up.

- Achieving mindfulness gives you the opportunity to examine your ideas and feelings without criticism, allowing for self-acceptance and empowering you with effective tools that can change negative thoughts into more optimistic ones.

- Practicing clear communication can be helpful in preventing overthinking and allowing you to express yourself in a non-judgmental way.

- Reconnecting with your values will help you stay true to yourself, think more clearly about your actions, and make decisions that are more aligned with your goals.

Chapter 6

Prioritizing Achieving Happiness in Relationships

The mark of a healthy, stable relationship is simple: happiness. A good relationship is one where you feel safe, secure, and happy. That does not mean being happy 24/7, of course. You and your partner are bound to have disagreements or even arguments sometimes. Real life is not a fairytale, after all. So, it is perfectly natural for you to get upset, angry, confused, sad, and worried sometimes. But you should not be feeling like that all the time. If you are constantly mired in negative thoughts and therefore negative feelings, then that means one of two things: either you are in a toxic relationship—in which case you need to get yourself out—or you have become caught in the overthinking loop, in which case you need to break the said loop. But how can you tell the difference? How can you know, for sure, that you are overthinking and ruminating and are not just stuck in a bad relationship? The answer to that question is simple: you can do so by questioning your very thoughts.

Questioning Your Thoughts

Questioning your thoughts is a perfect way of seeing whether the thoughts that are rushing through your head are real or not. As such, it can be a perfect tool for recognizing when you are overthinking and getting yourself to stop. Remember how we said that your subconscious mind has trouble recognizing the difference between what's real and what's not? Well, this facet of your subconscious can cause you to take negative thoughts like "I'm a failure," or "I'm unlovable" and accept them as hard-core facts. By now, you can probably see how this would put you into a negative mindset, increasing overthinking habits.

Questioning your thoughts is a way of challenging your mindset and such thought patterns. To that end, there are various questions you can ask yourself, starting with, "Is this thought real?" (Flanagan, n.d.). A lot of the time, we make exaggerated negative statements about ourselves or the situation we are in when we are overthinking or ruminating. What's more, we don't even realize that we are doing it. When something goes wrong, for instance, we adopt the kind of attitude where everything always goes wrong. We let the momentary negativity affect our interpretation of reality as it is. Admittedly, it can be rather hard to spot when we are doing this. Hence the question, "Is this real?"

Perhaps a more accurate version of this question would be, "Is this *always* real?" Think about it like this when you feel an emotion, like happiness or sadness, you don't feel it perpetually. You feel happy or angry for a period of time, then you move on and feel something else. The same goes for the different situations you might find yourself in. Say that you made a mistake. Does that mean that you made a mistake this one time or does it mean that you are always making mistakes, every moment of every day? It is the former, right? Yet, when you make a mistake, one of the first thoughts to pop into your mind is probably, "Why do I always do this?" Asking the question "Is this real?" or "Is this always real?" can be very effective in this situation. It can make you realize that your perception of reality in that moment is not reality itself. That realization can help you move on to other thoughts and move away from the negative thought loop where you keep blaming yourself (Plamondon-Thomas, 2021).

Another great question you can ask yourself to challenge your negative thoughts is "How would I feel and react when I believe this thought?" This question can be fantastic for recognizing the effects that negative thoughts and overthinking has on you and your relationship. It can help you to become more aware of the emotional reactions you give to these thoughts and the behaviors that they lead to. In other words, it can draw your attention directly to the damage your thoughts are doing to you and your relationship. Once you consciously bring these things to your attention, stopping the pattern that you are engaged in becomes easier. This is a bit like going full speed on an open road and suddenly hitting the brakes when the light unexpectedly turns from green to red. It will not be easy to do and will be jarring, to say the least, but it can shake you out of this self-damaging habit that you are in.

A good question to take this a step further is, "How would I feel or react if I did not believe this thought?" By asking this, you can evaluate your triggers, emotions, and emotional responses more objectively. You can see how different your emotional reality would be if you were to stop engaging in your current thought processes. As a result, you would be more willing to take a step back and try some of the positive mindset techniques, like positive self-affirmations and positive self-talk, that we have seen so far in this book.

As you are answering this question, "How would I feel or react if I did not believe this thought?" try to actually imagine how it would play out. This is called visualization. Visualization is a powerful mental tool that can help you to switch from negative thoughts and beliefs to positive ones. It can do so because your unconscious mind will take this figment of your imagination as reality and respond to it accordingly. But that is the only reason why visualization can help you challenge your negative thoughts. There is also the fact that this practice lays out scenarios alternative to the one that you have been imagining before you and makes them clear as day. It makes them more visible to you, which they will not be if you allow yourself to be swept away by catastrophizing scenarios, such as "My partner is going to leave me after this," or "They must be cheating on me." Put simply, then visualization, as part of challenging your thoughts, can make the things that were previously invisible to you visible and much easier to spot. This can, in turn, make taking a pause and adjusting your mindset a far easier feat to accomplish.

As you are questioning your thoughts and challenging your beliefs, it is important that you keep reminding yourself your thoughts are not objective facts. They are subjective representations of yourself or the situation you are in. That is good news because representations are based wholly on your perception of things (Lewis, 2019). Change your perception, that is to say, your mindset, and you can change a thought. Change your perception and you can go from, "the glass is half full" to "the glass is half empty" or "I'm unlovable," to "I'm a loveable human being and I love myself."

Meditation

So far, we have talked about meditation a couple of times in this book and there is a very simple reason for that: meditation is one of the best tools in your toolkit for stopping overthinking. Contrary to what you might think, meditation is not about controlling your thoughts. Instead, it is about allowing whatever thoughts you have to drift in and out of your mind without chasing after them.

No matter what you do, you will never be able to stop the negative thoughts, or any other kind of thought for that matter, from popping into your mind. That is not something you have control over. What you do have control over is how you react to those thoughts. When a negative thought pops into your mind, you can choose to do one of two things. You can follow after it and allow it to generate more and more negative thoughts and scenarios, or you can let it go.

Meditation is a mindfulness practice that teaches you how to simply be in the moment. It is a practice that shows you how to become fully aware of your feelings and thoughts, as well as the sensations you are feeling and the things you are experiencing. Being able to do all of these things requires directing your attention to them, instead of keeping them on negative thoughts and thought loops. This is the very thing that meditation teaches you to do. This, however, is neither an easy nor a quick skill to master.

A lot of people who struggle with overthinking often find meditation to be a difficult practice to begin and to stick with, for that matter. This is because letting go of negative thoughts without following after them is a bit like trying to ignore a car horn blaring incessantly right outside your window. The loud noise that the horn makes keeps drawing your attention to it, after all. But imagine that that car horn has been going off for the past 30 minutes or even two hours. After a certain point, you are going to stop hearing it. True, it is going to be annoying at first, and turning your attention away from the horn and back to your work will be a challenge. Sure, your attention will be drawn to it again, every once in a while, for a couple of minutes at a time. But the point is, you will be able to refocus on the assignment and stop hearing the horn. Then, after say, three hours have gone by, you will suddenly realize that not only have you stopped hearing the horn, but the sound itself has stopped. This is exactly what meditation can help you to achieve, except you have to substitute the horn for negative thoughts and overthinking and the car as your own mind.

What if you are one of those people that struggle with meditation though? Is it possible for you to stick with the practice regardless and eventually reap its benefits? Of course, it is, and doing so will not even take as much time as you think it will. At least, not when you make use of certain tricks of the trade.

One thing you can do to make it easier for you to get into and stick with meditation is to try to meditate at the same time every day (Garone, 2021). Some people prefer meditating in the morning, as it is a calm way of starting off the day and getting into the right mindset for it. Others prefer to do so at night, as it is a good way of winding down. Figure out what works best for you and your daily schedule, then stick with it. That means you should meditate every single day, assuming you want the practice to yield actual results.

Obviously, you should always be comfortable when you are meditating, meaning you should either be sitting or lying down in some comfortable spot. If you are not comfortable, then focusing on your breaths, bodily sensations, and the thoughts and feelings you experience in that moment—without chasing after them—will be impossible. In keeping with that, you should also try to meditate in a comfortable, relatively organized space. If you are meditating next to a pile of dirty laundry for instance, or in view of the trash you forgot to take out, you are probably going to get distracted.

If sitting still for extended periods of time is a challenge for you, then you should ease into meditation. You can start by meditating for just a few minutes for about a week or so, making sure to meditate every day. Then you should up your meditation time to 10 minutes, and keep it at that for another week (or a bit longer than that, if you would like). A week after that you can up it to 15 minutes, then 20, until you can meditate for at least 30 minutes in one sitting.

To make things even easier for yourself, you should meditate with a guided meditation app of some sort—there are a lot of them out there. This can give you a sense of direction and you will not have to worry about whether you are doing it right or not. While you are at it, you should keep your meditation practices confined to controlled breathwork. It is a scientifically proven fact that the simple act of taking deep, slow, regular breaths can calm down your nervous system and thus, settle your worries and lower your anxiety and stress levels. This is why there are many meditation techniques that focus solely on breathing. The point of breathing meditations is to turn your attention, fully and wholly onto your breath. This diverts your attention from the negative thoughts crowding your mind, of course, and makes letting them drift away easier to do (Zaccaro et al., 2018).

The key thing you must remind yourself of when meditating is that it is normal for your mind to wander from point to point. It is equally normal for negative thoughts to appear in your mind. As we said before, you can't stop negative thoughts from materializing, but you can stop yourself from pursuing them, and therein lies the power meditation wields against overthinking.

Re-Aligning Your Goals

Remember that exercise you did to discover what your core values were? Well, your core values are great tools to use for identifying your goals. Some people find themselves overthinking because they have difficulty understanding what it is they want. If you don't know what you want out of a relationship, for instance, you can't exactly ask for it. You can't communicate clearly with your partner about what you want or need. If you work on identifying your goals though, you can both understand and express such things. In doing so, you can stop your unmet needs and unrealized goals from turning into negative thought loops keeping you up at night.

The first step to goal setting, as always, is to identify whatever negative thoughts you are having. Take a closer look at your negative thoughts, without validating them, and see what exactly they are about. Are they about your current relationship status? Are they concerned about how secure you feel in your relationship? Are they more about trust? Are they about your and your partner's ability to openly and positively communicate with one another?

Once you have identified what lies at the core of your negative thoughts—communication issues, trust issues, intimacy issues, etc.—you need to ask yourself what needs to happen for that issue to be resolved. Let's say you and your partner are having communication issues and you saw that that issue lies at the epicenter of your negative thoughts. What needs to happen for this situation to change? Obviously, you need to have a calm but a deep conversation with your partner about your communication issues. That right there is the goal that you want to meet. This is because that is the goal that will help you to solve the issue you have been having and meet a previously unmet need. Your rumination habit will not disappear until and unless you take action to meet your needs, which entails setting goals for yourself.

For goals to be effective, they need to meet certain criteria. Otherwise, all the goals-setting in the world will not help you to resolve your rumination habit. For a goal to be considered a "good" one, it has to be (Mind Tools Content Team, 2022):

- Specific
- Measurable
- Achievable
- Relevant
- Time-bound

Hence the acronym "SMART." Making goals specific is a good idea because it gives you a concrete idea about what you want to achieve. This in turn makes creating a plan of action to meet that goal easy to do. "Talk to my partner about our communication issues," for instance, is not a good goal, because it is not very specific. "Talk to my partner this Thursday about their difficulty opening up to me and my finding it hard to make time to talk," for instance is very specific.

For a goal to be measurable, it has to be either motivating or meaningful in some way. "Have dinner together on Friday," might be a goal, but it is not all that motivating or meaningful (not that spending time with your partner is not meaningful). A goal about fixing the communication issues you have been having with your partner, on the other hand, as in the example earlier? That is a very motivating and meaningful goal because its ideal end result is to fix the communication between you and the person you love and improve your relationship.

For a goal to be achievable, meanwhile, it has to be realistic. Otherwise, you will not be able to realize it and will end up feeling dejected and upset as a result. Hence, you should always ask yourself whether or not you can actually accomplish a goal—any goal—that you have set for yourself after you have decided on it. If you truly believe that you can, then that could be an achievable goal. If, however, you are hesitant about how achievable it is, then it might be time to re-evaluate it.

A relevant goal is one that is going to be worth the effort you will put into achieving it. It is great that you want to fix the communication issues you have with your partner. But what if they don't want to put in the effort that is necessary for doing it? What if they choose to ignore the issue at hand, no matter how much you try to talk to them about it? If that is the case, then perhaps your goal should not be to keep trying to fix your relationship. Relationships need two people to work, after all, and if you are the only one who's willing to put the necessary work in? Well, then, unfortunately, it might be time to walk away.

Finally, for a task to be effective, it needs to be time-bound. That means you need to give yourself a certain timeline to complete your goal. If your goal is to talk to your partner about your issues, then it is vital to set a deadline for it. Otherwise, pushing off the talk and making excuses as to why you can't have it that day or that week becomes far too easy. Giving yourself a deadline, though, puts some mild pressure on you to actually accomplish your goal and thus, makes it far more likely that you will achieve it.

Key Takeaways

- The key to a strong and lasting relationship is happiness, and a solid relationship should give you the feeling of security, safety, and joy.

- Questioning your thoughts is a great technique for recognizing when you are overthinking and preventing the cycle from continuing.

- Meditation is a powerful tool that can help you break the cycle of overthinking and gain insight into your emotions, thoughts, physical sensations, and experiences. Through meditation practice, you can learn how to remain aware of yourself in any given moment.

- Uncovering your core values can be an invaluable asset when it comes to determining what you want and need out of life.

- Creating achievable goals is the only way to effectively

break a cycle of rumination. To make sure your objectives are attainable, they should follow the SMART criteria – specific, measurable, action-oriented, relevant, and time-bound.

Chapter 7

How to End a Toxic Relationship

When you finally manage to put an end to overthinking and rumination, you are left with one thing: clarity. Sometimes the clarity you attain allows you to figure out what you need to do to fix any relationship issues that you might be facing. Other times, though, clarity might allow you to see that saving your relationship is not really possible. It may even help you see that your current relationship is an inherently toxic one, hence the negative emotions and thoughts that it drags you into. The thing about toxic relationships is that, unlike healthy relationships, they are not salvageable.

If you come to realize that you are in a toxic relationship, there really is only one thing that you can do and that is to leave. This is because a toxic relationship is something that can be incredibly damaging to you, as a person. A toxic relationship can be defined as one that makes you feel that you are always misunderstood and unsupported (Scott, 2020). It is also one where you are under constant attack—be it verbal or even physical—and belittled and demeaned. As you can imagine, such treatment in a supposedly loving relationship can take a significant toll on your emotional and mental health, as well as your self-esteem.

Common Red Flags to Look Out For

So, how can you tell whether or not your relationship is toxic? First of all, it must be remembered that having relationship issues does not automatically translate to being in a toxic relationship. Every healthy relationship has its ups and downs and every couple faces their own, unique challenges. If you want to tell whether you are in a healthy relationship but going through a rough patch, or in a wholly unhealthy one, you must first curb your overthinking habits. This way, you can begin to evaluate your relationship and your feelings objectively and in the right mindset. Having done that, you can try to see if your relationship exhibits the signs that a typical toxic relationship will have.

There are numerous signs, or red flags, if you will, indicating that you are in a toxic relationship. The most blatantly obvious of these signs is physical or verbal, that is to say emotional, abuse (Scott, 2020). Unfortunately, not all red flags are as obvious as these. Some can be harder to see, as though there is a cloud bank surrounding the flag, making it challenging for you to spot its color. Once you quiet the din in your mind and truly focus, though? At that point, they start becoming more obvious.

Without further ado then, if you are exhibiting any of the following behaviors, then that means you are in a toxic relationship and it may be time to get out (Scott, 2020):

- Feeling angry, depressed, dejected, or exhausted (emotionally or physically and sometimes both) every time you speak with your partner.

- Your levels of self-esteem getting lower and lower over time, sometimes until you look up one day and can't quite pinpoint how your confidence got to be so low.

- Giving more than you are getting from your partner, on an emotional, mental, or material level, seeing as a healthy relationship is one where both parties try to give and take equally.

- Often feeling disrespected by your partner or like they are looking down on you.

- Having to walk on eggshells on the time and constantly being on edge, for fear of inciting their ire, irritation, or drawing their fire your way.

- Being unwilling to express your own opinions, thoughts, and feelings to your partner, or anyone else when they are around, especially if what you want to express is not what they believe in.

- Being afraid of or unwilling to be who you really are when you are with your partner, sometimes to the point where you do things you don't want to do or don't believe in (like things that clash with your own values), because they want it.

- Allowing your partner to bring out the worst in you, rather than the best, which is what should happen in a healthy relationship.

- Expending a great deal of emotional and mental energy to take care of their emotional well-being (more so than they do for you) and having to do so all the time to cheer them up and make them feel better. In other words, being responsible for your partner's entire emotional well-being.

- Always being blamed for things that go wrong or for mistakes, even when they are not your fault, and becoming accustomed to taking on the blame, to the extent that you start blaming yourself for various things as well.

Put in writing like this, it is easy to see how debilitating and exhausting any one of these things could be for a person who is experiencing them. Given that, if you yourself can observe these signs in yourself, it is vital that you end your relationship for your own well-being. To do that though, you will need to put a solid plan in place.

Leaving a Toxic Relationship

Deciding to end a relationship, any kind of relationship, is not an easy thing to do. But sometimes, as in the case of toxic relationships, it is necessary for your own health, happiness, and well-being. Once you have decided to end a toxic relationship, the first thing you need to do is to put a plan of action in place. This is especially true for cases where you worry about how your partner will react to the news. For starters, decide when you are going to end the relationship and how you are going to end it. Think about what you want to say to end the relationship and what you want to communicate. Save some money for when you do leave, especially if you had joint finances till now. If you are living with the person you are in a relationship with, figure out where you (or they) are going to go post-breakup. Make sure you have a place to go to, be it a hotel, or good friend's couch, or even your childhood bedroom at your parents' place when you leave. Let close, trusted people in your support circle know about your decision so that they can help you plan.

Once you have broken up with your partner, make sure to cut off all contact with them. More likely than not, you will miss them from time to time and want to call or text them. It is important that you don't do this or even respond to their texts and messages. Otherwise, you run the risk of being sucked right back into your old relationship and its toxic patterns. To prevent that, block your "ex's" number on your phone and unfollow them on social media (Rahman, 2022). This way, you can reduce any temptation you might be feeling, significantly.

To further ward off temptation, remind yourself that you deserve much better than what you got in this relationship. Honestly evaluate your needs and try to understand why you fell into a toxic relationship to begin with. This does not mean berating yourself for your choices and decisions, mind you. It simply means making an honest effort to understand their root causes and how they led you to the emotional, cognitive, and relationship patterns that you found yourself in. Put another way, it means using your self-awareness skills, which you have been developing, to understand yourself better.

Now, you might find yourself hesitating and facing various barriers when working on your exit plan, which will lead you out of your toxic relationship. This is perfectly normal. Just because a relationship was toxic, after all, does not mean you did not or don't care about the person you were in it with. That being said, you need to know what these barriers are and how to overcome them, if you are actually using your exit strategy. To that end, let's go over the most common barriers to leaving a toxic relationship and how to overcome them (Rahman, 2022):

- **Isolation**. A lot of the time, toxic relationships cause us to grow apart, stop talking to, or disconnect from our friends and even family members. This can result in a deep sense of isolation. It can also create the perception that you will be all alone if you leave your current partner. Overcoming this barrier starts with reaching out to just one person, who you know cares about you, while you are still in the relationship but are contemplating leaving.

This could be a sibling, for instance, or another family member, whose support you know you can rely on. It can also be a former best friend that you haven't spoken with in a while. By making an effort to reconnect with just a few, key people, you can remind yourself that you are not as alone as you have come to feel. You can also start building bridges and relationships with people you value once more. These people can become a very powerful support system that can be there for you both while you leave your relationship and afterward.

- **Fear**. This is a very important barrier to leaving and can take many shapes and forms. You may be afraid of how your partner will react when you tell them you are leaving, for instance. You may be afraid of hurting them. You may also be afraid that you will not find anyone else that is willing to love you. If you are afraid of your partner's reactions, then it is vital that you leave your relationship without telling them face to face. It is equally vital that they don't know where you go and that you cut off all contact and take measures such as blocking their number. If you are afraid of other things, like hurting them, then you need to remind yourself, over and over again, if need be, that you are not in charge of anyone's emotions, but your own. Your priority is to tend to your emotional well-being, and that is what you are doing by leaving. Finally, if you are afraid of not finding anyone else to love you, you need to work on changing that negative self-talk into positive self-talk and remind yourself that you are worthy of love and a healthy relationship.

- **Hope that your partner or the relationship will change.** A lot of people, too many people, really, choose to stay in toxic relationships, hoping that their partners will change. Spoiler alert: they will not. This vain hope keeps them in their relationships for longer than they should. The additional time that they spend in their toxic relationships takes more of a toll on their well-being, self-esteem, and mental health. Remind yourself of that fact when you hesitate and think, "But maybe next time will be different." The sad truth is the next time will not be different and your partner likely will not change. You do not have the power to control their decisions or actions. You only have the power to control your own. In this regard, you have all the power and you need to exercise this. So, take a deep breath and use your self-affirmations to also remind yourself of how strong and capable you truly are and let go of the false hope you have been clinging to. Then, take the steps necessary to walk away.

How to Break Up with Someone Compassionately

Assuming that you don't fear your partner's reaction, the breakup is something you want to handle face to face. It is also something that is nerve-wracking for even the best of us. You typically want to handle the breakup in a compassionate way, so as to hurt the person you are leaving as little as humanly possible. This is still a person you care about, after all, even if you are ending things with them.

So, how do you end a relationship compassionately? Your first step is to actually prepare for it, like you would for any important conversation. Your break-up speech shouldn't be filled with empty words and meaningless platitudes that anyone can use, like "It is not you, it is me." Instead, it should convey the reasons why you are ending the relationship clearly, concisely, and without laying blame on anyone. As you will remember "I feel statements—or "I felt" statements as the case may be—are great for this. You should think carefully, then, about what it is you want to say and how you want to end things. You should also give some thought to how you want to communicate that your decision to end things is not up for discussion. When stating this, you want to strike a line between compassionate and firm. Doing all of that will take some practice.

Your journal can be a great place for getting that practice. You can start by writing down your reasons for leaving and pouring everything you want out on the page. How can you sum up what you have written so that it is short and to the point, but still compassionate? You don't have to write down multiple drafts or anything like that. But you can use what you have written in your journal to mentally edit and prepare what you want to say. Once you have figured that out, you can physically practice what you want to say, in front of a mirror, perhaps, or with a friend. Doing this can help you manage your nerves a lot and make having the actual break-up conversation easier.

Speaking of nerves, another way of soothing them might be to think about what responses your partner might try to give to your reasons for ending things (Marin, 2015). This is especially important if you think your partner will try to get you to give the relationship another chance. If you anticipate them doing that, you can decide on a firm way of saying no, like, "I'm sorry, but I've made up my mind," and stick to that script, if in fact, your ex does try to change your mind.

Once you have decided to end the relationship and prepared yourself for it, you should make sure to do it as quickly as you can. Remember how it was important for your goals to be time-bound? Well, it is important for your break-up to be time-bound as well, Otherwise, you might keep pushing it off. You might come up with all sorts of excuses as to why you can't break up with your partner today, and those excuses can cause you to drag things out. This can cause you to get angry at or upset with yourself, which can, you guessed it, make you start overthinking, which is one thing you want to avoid in this scenario. That being said, you should obviously be mindful of your timing. You would not want to break up with your partner on their birthday, for instance, immediately after their grandfather's funeral, or on New Year's Eve. Take major events like these into consideration as you are planning how and when you want to end your relationship.

A great way of ending a breakup conversation is to thank your partner. Relationships, even toxic ones, have a lot to teach us. We can learn a great deal about ourselves through our relationships. Acknowledging that to your partner and to yourself, and expressing your gratitude for the time that you spent together can really help soften the blow of a breakup. It can help the person opposite you to feel just a little bit better. Of course, you don't want to give your partner false hope and make them think that they can change your mind or that you will get back together in the future, when you are thanking them. That is why you should keep your "thank you" short and to the point, just as you should keep your break-up speech short and to the point. That way, you can essentially rip off the Band-Aid and make it easier for the both of you to move on.

Coping with the Aftermath of a Toxic Relationship

Just because a relationship was toxic, does not mean you won't be dealing with some heartbreak and grief after it is over. Not only is it expected for you to feel such things, but it is also very normal. Given that, you should never berate yourself for grieving for a relationship. Instead, you should allow yourself to feel all that you feel and even make an effort to explore them further.

A great way of understanding and processing your post-break-up emotions is to keep a log of them or to journal about them (Lamoreux, 2021). True, you might not exactly feel like writing about your feelings. But you should do so anyway, as it has some serious long-term benefits for your emotional and mental well-being. For instance, journaling about your emotions can reduce the amount of stress and anxiety you are under, which likely will be a lot (Baikie

& Wilhelm, 2005). By processing what you are feeling, bit by bit, every day, you can prevent negative emotions and thoughts from making you question your decisions. You can consciously remind yourself of why you made this decision and fortify your resolve to stick to it, even as you grieve.

One thing that everyone who goes through a breakup experience is how much free or empty time they suddenly have. That is the time that they used to spend with their partner. This is something that you will undoubtedly experience for yourself and when you do, you will probably be a little baffled. I mean, how are you supposed to spend that time now? Well, you should spend it filling it up with all sorts of different things, like hanging out with your friends and loved ones, engaging in hobbies you actually like, going for a walk, working out, or trying to pick up a new hobby. Doing things like this can help you to cultivate more positive emotions following your break and keep you from being idle, which is usually when the temptation to reach out to your ex kicks in.

While doing things like pursuing your hobbies and interests are great, the importance of turning to your friends and family, that is to say, your support system, cannot be overstated in the post-break-up period (Lamoreux, 2021). Your support system is made up of individuals that can hold your hand while you weep, talk things through with you, and cheer you up when you need it. They are essential for you as you rebuild your single life, reconnect with yourself, and figure out where you want to go from here. Turning to your support system while managing the aftermath of your breakup keeps you from feeling like you are isolated and alone. Thus, it keeps negative thoughts at bay, and helps you to combat them, and overthinking.

Your support system and journaling habits can help you to combat one other, potentially debilitating feeling: guilt. Guilt can be a truly crippling thing and you might experience it for all sorts of reasons post-breakup. You might be feeling guilty that you hurt your partner, for instance. Alternatively, you might be feeling guilty because you believe you stayed in that relationship for longer than you should have. Whatever the source of your guilt is, you need to work through it actively and consciously and ultimately forgive yourself. Otherwise, you will neither be able to move past it nor will you really be able to move on. If guilt is something you especially struggle with, you might want to consider seeking therapy to process it. Therapists can be great for helping us to realize the root causes of various feelings and guilt is no exception. Talking with a therapist of some sort, then, can be a very effective way of learning how to forgive yourself and stop taking on the blame for everything.

A last thing to keep in mind when navigating your post-break-up phase is that you should be sure to make time for yourself and treat yourself. Treating yourself by, say, putting on some soothing music and relaxing, enjoying a slice of that cake you really wanted, or filling up the tub and soaking in it may not seem all that important to you. But these are all acts of self-care when you think about it, and self-care is an expression of self-love. Practicing self-love is a great way of reminding yourself that you are deserving of love and care and you don't have to turn to outside sources to get it. Being in a relationship can be great, but your first and most valuable relationship is the one you have with yourself. As such, you should treat yourself with the care that you deserve. This can be a great way of supporting yourself as you heal and strengthen your positive mindset. It can help you reconnect with who you are and discover your hidden depths.

Key Takeaways

- If you are in a toxic relationship, there are typically signs that will indicate this. The more apparent red flags include physical or verbal abuse.

- Taking the courageous step to end an unhealthy relationship requires you to develop a plan of action and stay true to it.

- To break free from a detrimental relationship, it is essential to identify the common barriers as well as develop effective strategies to overcome them.

- A wonderful way to bring closure to relationships, even those that are toxic and unhealthy, is expressing gratitude for the life lessons they have brought.

- Nurturing yourself with self-love is an effective way to remind you that your worthiness of care and compassion comes from within, not from anyone or anything else.

Conclusion

Overthinking and rumination are habits that many of us—most of us if we are being honest—have. They are habits that we have grown so used to that we no longer realize how damaging they can be for us and for the relationship we are in. The fact of the matter is, though, overthinking is probably one of the worst things we can do for our emotional health and the well-being of our relationships.

Overthinking is something that is born out of relationship anxieties. You might have relationship anxieties for a variety of reasons, from past negative experiences to insecure attachment styles. Whatever the case may be, you need to identify what those root causes are if you want to resolve your anxieties and your overthinking habits once and for all. Otherwise, those anxieties that you feel can prime your behavior in a number of ways, such as by causing you to sabotage your own relationship and misinterpret your partner's motives and actions.

One of the gravest problems with relationship anxiety is that it leads to overthinking, which can be incredibly damaging to your mental and physical health. From causing cardiovascular diseases to lowering your immune system and leading to depressive disorders, overthinking can truly wreak havoc in your body and life. It can deal major blows to your self-esteem as well.

Similarly, relationship anxiety can lead to rumination, which is equally as damaging as overthinking, if not more so. Ironically, rumination is something many people engage in to solve their problems. This proves an ineffective method of tackling problems though, be they personal ones or relationship issues. Rumination, which is caused by low self-esteem, can turn relationships toxic, weaken your ability to regulate and understand your own emotions, and communicate your needs.

All in all, then, overthinking and rumination are both habits that you should do your best to avoid. One way of doing this is working to improve and increase your self-awareness. Being a self-aware individual is essential for being able to have strong and healthy relationships, as you've seen. This is because a person who doesn't understand themselves, can neither communicate the things they need to their partner nor understand them fully. Luckily, there are an array of methods people can use to increase their self-awareness. From journaling to meditating and asking for constructive feedback from others, the possibilities are endless.

Interestingly enough a number of these methods can also help people to cultivate a positive mindset, which is very necessary for combating overthinking and rumination, seeing as both of these are fruits of negative mindsets. To cultivate a positive mindset, you need to work on four specific things: nurturing positivity itself, turning to mindfulness, practicing clear communication, and reconnecting with your values. Using exercises and practices that help improve these four aspects, such as using positive self-talk, relying on "I statements" when communicating with others, and doing body scans, can turn the volume of negative thoughts down while turning up the sound of positive ones. This naturally helps you to form a positive mindset, which you can use to cultivate a healthy relationship.

A healthy relationship is obviously one where you feel safe, secure, and happy. Achieving such a relationship requires combating the negative thoughts that may pop into your head, which they will do. Like with developing a positive mindset, there are multiple ways you can go about doing this as well. Questioning the reality of your thoughts and challenging them, for instance, is one of them. So is practicing meditation, particularly mindfulness meditation. These kinds of practices and exercises can make recognizing the things that make you happy in a relationship and the things that you need far easier. Once you recognize these, you can consciously voice them and once you voice them, you and your partner can start working together to fix whatever relationship issues you might have.

That said, some relationships are next to impossible to fix, no matter how hard you try. These are decidedly toxic relationships and there's only one thing you can do in a toxic relationship: walk away. This is because toxic relationships are incredibly damaging to you, as an individual. They can whittle down your self-esteem and self-confidence levels and cause you a great deal of stress, anxiety, unhappiness, shame, guilt, and anger on a near-perpetual basis.

Since fixing toxic relationships isn't really possible, recognizing them for what they are and knowing when to walk away are vital. To walk away from a toxic relationship you will need to put some kind of plan of action into place. You will need to turn to your support system, know exactly where you're going to go before you leave, and make a commitment to stay away once you have ended the relationship.

Of course, ending a toxic relationship doesn't mean you aren't allowed to grieve for it. Nor does it mean you cannot handle the breakup in a compassionate way. The best strategy to adopt when handling break-up conversations is to keep them short and clear and strike a fine line between being compassionate and firm. Thanking your partner at the end of the breakup speech and preparing for the conversation in advance can be fantastic ways of achieving both.

Of course, having read the entirety of *Fix Overthinking in Relationships* you already know all this. You also now know how to recognize the signs of things like overthinking, relationship anxiety, rumination, and toxic relationships. That being the case, the only thing left for you to do is to look inside yourself. Do you recognize any of these signs that have been discussed at length in this book? If so, it's time for you to get to work, so that you obtain the kind of happiness and peace of mind you want and deserve in your daily life, as well as your relationship.

Thank you for reading *Fix Overthinking in Relationships*. I hope you have enjoyed the book. If you have, please leave a review!

About the Author

Edgar struggled with severe shyness and lack of self-confidence growing up, which compelled him not to express himself in school for most of his childhood. Despite his straight A's in high school, he felt he had nothing to offer the world. The stress of self-doubt and the fear of rejection caused him to lose interest in human connection, which is important for living a meaningful and happy life. Without the necessary support system, Edgar was left with no guidance. This resulted in slow growth and a lack of motivation, which later set off anxiety and depression.

He knew that he had a problem and needed help but did not know where to begin or who could help him. He turned to books, seminars, and courses. It wasn't until he started applying everything he had learned that his personal transformation finally ensued.

After a series of successes in relationships and career, Edgar began writing books for people who were dealing with similar problems he once had. He started by researching methods to help himself, and he now has a deep understanding of how other people can be helped as well. He discovered his passion for assisting others in coping with the same issues. He dedicated himself to researching and sharing techniques to help others improve their lives in a variety of approaches, using both personal experience and scientific research.

As a writer on the topic of self-help and self-improvement, he has helped many people learn how to better take care of their lives, improve their well-being, and build meaningful relationships. His work discusses how to lead an emotionally healthy life and be on better terms with oneself, thus improving one's relationships with others. He is always looking for new ways to improve his own life and the lives of others. He provides tips and resources in areas such as self-care, self-confidence, and communication.

He enjoys taking walks, cooking healthy food, listening to audiobooks, and hanging out with friends and family in his spare time.

Check out more books on his Amazon profile - https://www.amazon.com/author/edgarwise

Leaving a Review

As an independent author with limited marketing resources, reviews for my books are essential in order to survive as an indie writer. New works of literature get published daily, so there's no guarantee that any given work will be successful. Your review can help authors like me grow and share their knowledge with more people.

If you enjoyed this book, I would really appreciate your honest feedback. You can leave a review by going to this book's page on Amazon. Your feedback is important to me so I can find out what you like and don't, which in turn helps me make better decisions about my writing style.

Thank you for your support,

Edgar

References

Ackerman, C. (2017, January 18). 22 mindfulness exercises, techniques & activities for adults (+ PDF's). PositivePsychology.com. https://positivepsychology.com/mindfulness-exercises-techniques-activities/

Ackerman, C. (2018, July 5). *What is positive mindset: 89 ways to achieve a positive mental attitude.* PositivePsychology.com. https://positivepsychology.com/positive-mindset/

Ackerman, C. E. (2019, April 9). *Mindfulness and positive psychology: A look at the benefits and links.* PositivePsychology.com. https://positivepsychology.com/mindfulness-positive-psychology-3-great-insights/

Admin, M. (2016, August 31). *How neuroscience can help us give and receive critical feedback*. IMPACT: Monash Business School. https://impact.monash.edu/leadership/how-neuroscience-can-help-us-give-and-receive-critical-feedback/

Alloway, T. (2022, September 19). *Is overthinking the cornerstone of depression?* Psychology Today. https://www.psychologytoday.com/intl/blog/keep-it-in-mind/202209/is-overthinking-the-cornerstone-depression

American Psychiatric Association. (2020, March 5). *Rumination: A cycle of negative thinking*. Www.psychiatry.org. https://www.psychiatry.org/News-room/APA-Blogs/Rumination-A-Cycle-of-Negative-Thinking#:~:text=Rumination%20involves%20repetitive%20thinking%20or

American Psychological Association. (2023). *Someone to complain with isn't necessarily a good thing, especially for teenage girls*. Apa.org. https://www.apa.org/news/press/releases/2007/07/co-rumination

Arlin Cuncic. (2018, February 12). *How self-esteem affects social anxiety disorder*. Verywell Mind. https://www.verywellmind.com/self-esteem-and-social-anxiety-4158220

Baikie, K. A., & Wilhelm, K. (2005). Emotional and physical health benefits of expressive writing. *Advances in Psychiatric Treatment*, 11(5), 338–346. https://doi.org/10.1192/apt.11.5.338

Better Health. (2014). *Relationships and communication*. Vic.gov.au. https://www.betterhealth.vic.gov.au/health/healthyliving/relationships-and-communication

Betz, M. (2021, April 21). *What is self-awareness, and why is it important?* Www.betterup.com. https://www.betterup.com/blog/what-is-self-awareness

Brooks-Gunn, J., & Lewis, M. (1984). The development of early visual self-recognition. *Developmental Review*, 4(3), 215–239. https://doi.org/10.1016/s0273-2297(84)80006-4

Caporuscio, J. (2020, April 1). *Relationship anxiety: Signs, causes, and management*. Www.medicalnewstoday.com. https://www.medicalnewstoday.com/articles/relationship-anxiety#treatment

Cascio, C. N., O'Donnell, M. B., Tinney, F. J., Lieberman, M. D., Taylor, S. E., Strecher, V. J., & Falk, E. B. (2015). Self-affirmation activates brain systems associated with self-related processing and reward and is reinforced by future orientation. *Social Cognitive and Affective Neuroscience*, 11(4), 621–629. https://doi.org/10.1093/scan/nsv136

Cherry, K. (2020, July 14). *What is self-awareness?* Verywell Mind. https://www.verywellmind.com/what-is-self-awareness-2795023

Cirino, E. (2018, May 24). *10 tips to help you stop ruminating*. Healthline. https://www.healthline.com/health/how-to-stop-ruminating#causes

Cleaveland Clinic. (2022, May 17). *Overthinking disorder: is it a mental illness?* Cleveland Clinic. https://health.clevelandclinic.org/is-overthinking-a-mental-illness/#:~:text=Is%20overthinking%20a%20mental%20illness

Dolan, E. W. (2017, January 26). *Meditation training increases the ability to perceive the self in a more healthy, present-moment way.* PsyPost. https://www.psypost.org/2017/01/meditation-training-increases-ability-perceive-self-healthy-present-moment-way-47121

Dr. Batra. (n.d.). *Overthinking can mess with your health.* Dr Batra's™. https://www.drbatras.com/overthinking-can-mess-with-your-health#:~:text=It%20can%20suppress%20your%20immune

Eurich, T. (2018, January 4). *What self-awareness really is (and how to cultivate it).* Harvard Business Review. https://hbr.org/2018/01/what-self-awareness-really-is-and-how-to-cultivate-it

Flanagan, C. (n.d.). *The 4 questions that can defeat negative thoughts.* Oprah.com. https://www.oprah.com/omagazine/4-questions-that-defeat-negative-thoughts_1

Garone, S. (2021, April 2). *9 tips for meditating when you're an overthinker.* Healthline. https://www.healthline.com/health/mind-body/9-tips-for-meditating-when-youre-an-overthinker#Create-a-consistent-schedule

Gupta, A. (2022, April 29). *Are you stuck in the vicious cycle of overthinking? It's risky, warns an expert.* Healthshots. https://www.healthshots.com/mind/mental-health/heres-how-overthinking-can-impact-your-overall-health/

Habash, C. (2022, February 1). *What is self-reflection, and why is it important for self-improvement?* Thriveworks. Counseling and Life Coaching - Find a Counselor. https://thriveworks.com/blog/importance-self-reflection-improvement/

Hehir, J. (Director). (2020, May 17). The Last Dance. ESPN Films.

Iwanaga, M., Yokoyama, H., & Seiwa, H. (2004). Coping availability and stress reduction for optimistic and pessimistic individuals. *Personality and Individual Differences*, 36(1), 11–22. https://doi.org/10.1016/s0191-8869(03)00047-3

Jostmann, N. B., Karremans, J., & Finkenauer, C. (2011). When love is not blind: Rumination impairs implicit affect regulation in response to romantic relationship threat. *Cognition & Emotion*, 25(3), 506–518. https://doi.org/10.1080/02699931.2010.541139

Kirmayer, M. (2018, April 3). *How co-rumination turns healthy relationships toxic*. Psychology Today. https://www.psychologytoday.com/us/blog/casual-to-close/201804/how-co-rumination-turns-healthy-relationships-toxic#:~:text=Co%2Drumination%20involves%20repeatedly%20discussing

Lamoreux, K. (2021, July 22). *Just make it stop! 10 steps to end a toxic relationship*. Psych Central. https://psychcentral.com/blog/steps-to-end-a-toxic-relationship#log-emotions

Lewis, R. (2019, February 24). *What actually is a thought? And how is information physical?* Psychology Today.

https://www.psychologytoday.com/us/blog/finding-purpose/201902/what-actually-is-a-thought-and-how-is-information-physical

Lindsay, E. K., Chin, B., Greco, C. M., Young, S., Brown, K. W., Wright, A. G. C., Smyth, J. M., Burkett, D., & Creswell, J. D. (2018). How mindfulness training promotes positive emotions: Dismantling acceptance skills training in two randomized controlled trials. *Journal of Personality and Social Psychology*, 115(6), 944–973. https://doi.org/10.1037/pspa0000134

Lutz, J., Brühl, A. B., Scheerer, H., Jäncke, L., & Herwig, U. (2016). Neural correlates of mindful self-awareness in mindfulness meditators and meditation-naïve subjects revisited. *Biological Psychology*, 119, 21–30. https://doi.org/10.1016/j.biopsycho.2016.06.010

Ma, Z., & Zhang, N. (2021, June 4). *Default Mode Network - an overview*. ScienceDirect Topics. https://www.sciencedirect.com/topics/neuroscience/default-mode-network#:~:text=The%20default%20mode%20network%20(DMN

MalPaper. (2021, October 21). *Is there science behind positive daily affirmations?* Mål Paper. https://malpaper.com/blogs/news/is-there-science-behind-positive-daily-affirmations#:~:text=Studies%20prove%20that%20positive%20affirmations

Marin, V. (2015, November 30). *13 tips for breaking up with someone compassionately*. Bustle. https://www.bustle.com/articles/126171-13-tips-for-breaking-up-with-someone-compassionately

Mayo Clinic. (n.d.). *Inflammatory bowel disease (IBD) - Symptoms and causes*. Mayo Clinic. https://www.mayoclinic.org/diseases-conditions/inflammatory-bowel-disease/symptoms-causes/syc-20353315#:~:text=Inflammatory%20bowel%20disease%20(IBD)%20is

Mayo Clinic. (2018, May 4). *Anxiety disorders - symptoms and causes*. Mayo Foundation for Medical Education and Research. https://www.mayoclinic.org/diseases-conditions/anxiety/symptoms-causes/syc-20350961

Mayo Clinic. (2021). *High cholesterol - symptoms and causes*. Mayo Clinic. https://www.mayoclinic.org/diseases-conditions/high-blood-cholesterol/symptoms-causes/syc-20350800#:~:text=With%20high%20cholesterol%2C%20you%20can

Mead, E. (2019, September 26). *What is positive self–talk? (incl. examples)*. PositivePsychology.com. https://positivepsychology.com/positive-self-talk/

Mind Tools Content Team. (n.d.). *What are your values?* Www.mindtools.com. https://www.mindtools.com/a5eygum/what-are-your-values

Mind Tools Content Team. (2022). *SMART goals*. Www.mindtools.com. https://www.mindtools.com/a4wo118/smart-goals

Mishra, K. (2021, December 31). *Overthinking? Deal with it before it destroys your peace of mind.* Healthshots. https://www.healthshots.com/mind/mental-health/overthinking-and-its-impact-on-your-mental-health-know-from-an-expert/

Murray, S. L., Holmes, J. G., MacDonald, G., & Ellsworth, P. C. (1998). Through the looking glass darkly? When self-doubts turn into relationship insecurities. *Journal of Personality and Social Psychology*, 75(6), 1459–1480. https://doi.org/10.1037/0022-3514.75.6.1459

National Health Service. (2017, October 24). *Irritable bowel syndrome (IBS).* Nhs.uk. https://www.nhs.uk/conditions/irritable-bowel-syndrome-ibs/#:~:text=Irritable%20bowel%20syndrome%20(IBS)%20is

Olson, E. J. (2018 11). *Can lack of sleep make you sick?* Mayo Clinic. https://www.mayoclinic.org/diseases-conditions/insomnia/expert-answers/lack-of-sleep/faq-20057757#:~:text=Olson%2C%20M.D.

Osborn, S. (2020, September 21). *How to stop overthinking at night→5 proven strategies for sleep.* Samantha Osborne Therapy. https://samanthaosbornetherapy.com/blog/how-to-stop-overthinking-at-night

Plamondon-Thomas, N. (2021, June 28). *Overthinking part three: 5 questions to ask yourself.* LinkedIn. https://www.linkedin.com/pulse/overthinking-part-three-5-questions-ask-yourself-plamondon-thomas/

Plumptree, E. (2022, October 13). *Different ways to cope with relationship anxiety*. Verywell Mind. https://www.verywellmind.com/learning-how-to-cope-with-relationship-anxiety-5186885

Quora. (2016, October 21). *Where do our thoughts come from?* Forbes. https://www.forbes.com/sites/quora/2016/10/21/where-do-our-thoughts-come-from/?sh=21b50f472ee2

Rahman, I. (2022, August 26). *How to leave a toxic relationship*. Choosing Therapy. https://www.choosingtherapy.com/how-to-leave-a-toxic-relationship/

Raypole, C. (2019a, February 19). *Attachment theory: how your childhood impacts your relationships*. Healthline Media. https://www.healthline.com/health/attachment-disorder-in-adults

Raypole, C. (2019b, November 14). *Relationship anxiety: 16 signs and tips*. Healthline. https://www.healthline.com/health/relationship-anxiety#signs

Raypole, C. (2020, September 1). *Do affirmations work? Yes, but there's a catch*. Healthline. https://www.healthline.com/health/mental-health/do-affirmations-work#how-they-work

Reagan, A. J., Mitchell, L., Kiley, D., Danforth, C. M., & Dodds, P. S. (2016). The emotional arcs of stories are dominated by six basic shapes. *EPJ Data Science*, 5(1). https://doi.org/10.1140/epjds/s13688-016-0093-1

Rochat, P. (2003). Five levels of self-awareness as they unfold early in life. *Consciousness and Cognition*, 12(4), 717–731. https://doi.org/10.1016/s1053-8100(03)00081-3

Sadurní Rodríguez, Dr. G. (2020, October 16). *Rumination: when your thoughts don't have an off button*. The Psychology Group Fort Lauderdale. https://thepsychologygroup.com/ruminating-thoughts-and-anxiety/

Scott, E. (2019). *Rumination: Why do people obsess over things?* Verywell Mind. https://www.verywellmind.com/rumination-why-do-people-obsess-over-things-3144571

Scott, E. (2020, July 4). *What is a toxic relationship?* Verywell Mind. https://www.verywellmind.com/toxic-relationships-4174665#:~:text=A%20toxic%20relationship%20is%20one

Stephanie. (2022, September 20). *Overthinking vs. constructive problem solving*. Melli O'Brien. https://melliobrien.com/overthinking-vs-constructive-problem-solving/#:~:text=It%20actually%20makes%20you%20less

Tank, A. (2019, August 21). *Strategies to stop overthinking and start goal setting*. Entrepreneur. https://www.entrepreneur.com/leadership/strategies-to-stop-overthinking-and-start-goal-setting/336857

Tartakovsky, M. (2015, January 14). *Why do I ruminate? (and how to stop)*. Psych Central. https://psychcentral.com/blog/the-reasons-we-ruminate-and-how-to-reduce-the-cycle#3

therapist.com team. (2022, December 6). *What is self-esteem, and how can I improve mine?* Therapist.com . https://therapist.com/self-development/what-is-self-esteem/#:~:text=Levels%20of%20self%2Desteem

Times Entertainment Times. (2019, June 21). *Signs that overthinking is killing your relationship*. The Times of India. https://timesofindia.indiatimes.com/life-style/relationships/love-sex/signs-that-overthinking-is-killing-your-relationship/articleshow/69876481.cms#:~:text=Overthinking%20can%20make%20you%20assume

Torres, F. (2020, October). *What is depression?* Psychiatry; American Psychiatric Association. https://www.psychiatry.org/patients-families/depression/what-is-depression

Walsh, A. (2016, June 3). *How overthinking kills the creative process and 5 ways to prevent it*. Www.linkedin.com. https://www.linkedin.com/pulse/how-overthinking-kills-creative-process-5-ways-prevent-aviva-walsh/

Yale Medicine. (2022). *Chronic stress*. Yale Medicine. https://www.yalemedicine.org/conditions/stress-disorder#:~:text=%E2%80%A2A%20consistent%20sense%20of

Zaccaro, A., Piarulli, A., Laurino, M., Garbella, E., Menicucci, D., Neri, B., & Gemignani, A. (2018). How Breath-Control Can Change Your Life: A Systematic Review on Psycho-Physiological Correlates of Slow Breathing. *Frontiers in Human Neuroscience*, 12(353). https://doi.org/10.3389/fnhum.2018.00353

Zhou, H.-X., Chen, X., Shen, Y.-Q., Li, L., Chen, N.-X., Zhu, Z.-C., Castellanos, F. X., & Yan, C.-G. (2020). Rumination and the default mode network: Meta-analysis of brain imaging studies and implications for depression. *NeuroImage*, 206, 116287. https://doi.org/10.1016/j.neuroimage.2019.116287

Printed in Great Britain
by Amazon